A PLAY IN MUSIC

THE CRADLE WILL ROCK

BY

MARC BLITZSTEIN

RANDOM HOUSE · NEW YORK

Note

THE CRADLE WILL ROCK

is the sole property of the producer and the author, and is fully protected by copyright. It may not be acted, either by professionals or amateurs, without the payment of a royalty. Public readings and radio broadcastings are likewise forbidden. All inquiries concerning rights should be addressed to the producer, Mercury Theatre, 1430 Broadway, New York City.

The non-professional acting rights of *The Cradle Will Rock* are controlled exclusively by the New Theatre League, 132 West 43rd Street, New York City, without whose permission in writing no performance of it may be made.

MANUFACTURED IN THE UNITED STATES OF AMERICA

FOREWORD

by ARCHIBALD MacLEISH

It may be true that no man who does not love the world can write well or justly for the stage. But .it is certainly true that no man can write well or justly for the stage who does not hate the worldly audience and find means to destroy it. Until it is destroyed there can be no human touch between his work and the human minds he works for.

The worldly audience is not human. It is not a collection of men and women sitting in their seats. It is something very different. It is a creature in its own dimensions. It answers to the definition of the Tory who said, "Your people, Sir, your people is a great beast." Your audience is a great beast. It is a beast sensual, cruel, and alert. It is a beast that waits in darkness as the spider waits, watching the stir within a little shaft of light. It is a beast that hungers secretly as the panther hungers, stirring softly in the narrow room of its impatience. It is a beast that clamors greedily as the monkeys clamor, barking voraciously from safety in the trees. It is a beast of one desire and that desire is *to feel*.

If you are courageous and sleep well you may turn softly when the lights are down in any Broadway theatre and see this monster. It is a monster of many faces which are all one face; of many bodies which are all one body. It is a monster with the faces of ageing women, lewdness relaxing the corners of their loosened mouths, their collapsed breasts sighing, "Make me feel." It is a monster with the bodies of tired men, their shoulders back against the pliant plush, their knees thrust forward for the thoughts to touch them. It is a monster with the eyes of the defeated young: the young girls cheated of the moment when the world should have been real; the young men cheated of themselves and impotent in everything but malice.

It is this monster, this audience both greedy and inert, both impotent and sensual, that must be killed. It must be killed because so long as it lives in the dark silence of its seats nothing true or noble can be shown upon the stage. It must be killed because it is greedy only for its own gratification and because, being greedy, it hates and will destroy what cannot be devoured. Most of all it hates and will destroy a work of art. For a work of art is not a prey it can devour. A work of art is not a morsel of indulgence to be sucked between the teeth. A work of art is a hard and tooth-breaking fact, by no nerves or blood-vessels to be metabolized into gratification and satiety. A work of art is a finality as actual as a man: more actual than most. A work of art is a finality with which a man can only make his peace: with which a man alone and never an audience can find a peace to make.

6

What is necessary therefore for the playwright who wishes to write truly and honestly and in form of art is to destroy this audience. Which means to destroy its quality of audience and change it back to men and women who will think and judge. What is necessary is to change the audience to men and women and compel these men and women to make terms with what they see.

It is not an easy necessity nor is it one much urged upon the playwrights of our generation. With a few notable exceptions the critics who advise these playwrights advise them to reverse the honorable order. If terms are to be made, the play shall make them. And make them not with men as men but with the audience that bought the seats and sits there. If the audience will be amused (and it will be amused), let it have amusement on its own conditions. If the audience desires to be made to feel (and what else does the audience desire?), let it be made to feel until it is giddy.

The advice is given and the advice is taken, but the necessity remains. That it remains may be proved quite simply by the fact that two of the most eminent poets of our generation have obeyed it. Brecht obeyed it in his play *Mother*, which failed with more distinction in its Theatre Union production in New York than most successes gain in years of glory. Eliot obeyed it in his *Murder in the Cathedral*, which more and more emerges as the greatest play our generation has produced.

Brecht obeyed the necessity to eliminate the audience

by eliminating the theatre: He burned the house to get rid of the rats—but no one doubts that he got rid of them. The device was a brutal and entire destruction of the whole theatrical illusion. Eliot killed his audience more deftly. His device was the metamorphosis of the murderers who come forward out of time and stage and verse to justify their action after Thomas dies. But both devices were successful. The audience was destroyed and its members were sent out of the theatre with a sense of individual responsibility toward the play such as few of them had wished for and fewer still foreseen. Both plays carried beyond the greedy passivity, the receptive inertness of the audience to reach the active and participating minds of individual men.

Brecht and Eliot, however, are merely the most eminent of the assassins of the audience. They are not the most recent. Nor are they the most successful. The most successful must be put down as Marc Blitzstein. Mr. Blitzstein's operetta, *The Cradle Will Rock,* is direct enough, candid enough, and sharp enough to reduce any audience ever collected to its human components. Under Orson Welles' direction and John Houseman's production at the Mercury the present edition of the play is so unarguably a piece *of* theatre *for* theatre that the theatrical illusion—the illusion, that is, that what occurs upon the stage is "real"—never has a chance to establish itself. The actors are at all times actors: when they are not down stage acting they are at the back of the stage on their chairs. The play is at all times a play. And the effect upon the observer is the human and humanly becoming effect of the work of art upon the man who faces it.

But remarkable as is Mr. Blitzstein's success, more remarkable still is its history. The Mercury production of *The Cradle Will Rock* is not an arbitrary act of theatrical inventiveness. On the contrary the first production of the play as prepared for the Welles-Houseman Federal Theatre unit last spring was quite unlike the present production. It was the refusal of the Administratrix of the Arts Projects in Washington to permit the operetta to be given which brought about the present production, and the genius of the present production lies in the willingness of its director to accept the pattern of an accident and give it balanced form. When the Federal Theatre production was banned with the first-night audience already on the sidewalk in front of the Maxine Elliott, and when Welles and Houseman took over the play themselves, hired the Venice Theatre twenty blocks away, loaded an old piano into a truck and started off with their angry audience at their heels, they walked into the most exciting evening of theatre this New York generation has seen.

In an unaired theatre, on a stage illuminated by a couple of dusty spots, with a cast scattered through the audience (where a ruling of Equity kept it), and to the music of an upright piano manipulated by the composer in his shirt sleeves, there occurred a miracle. From the first voice of the first singer the thing was evident: There was no audience. There was instead a room full of men and women as eager in the play as any actor. As singers rose in one part and another of the auditorium the faces of these men and women made new and changing circles around them. They were well-wishing faces: human faces such as a man may sometimes see among partisans of the same cause or friends who hope good things for one another. The whole feel of the room was of well-wishing and common cause.

Upon that evening Mr. Welles built his Mercury production. For that evening made it very evident that the monstrous beast which devours plays and playwrights is a creature of the theatrical illusion which can be killed if the illusion can be killed. It is the pretense that a play is not a play but a bit of "real life" neatly made visible at the end of a longish room which breeds your audiences. It is this pretense which produces the characteristic, inert, receptive audience reaction. Because the audience is not supposed to be present it is not really present. Because the audience is supposed to be spying it does truly spy. Because the events which it watches are supposed to be real events happening somewhere else, it permits itself to be "carried away" and its total emotional experience is one of vicarious satisfaction broken by the kind of relief a man may have awakening from a dream. The fantastic exhibitionism of a typical New York first night is nothing but a childish attempt to compensate for the dream quality of the audience's actual rôle.

To destroy this exceptionally shopworn illusion and

set up a play for what it is—a play—means principally to restore to the audience its dignity and self-respect and association with life. It is usually assumed that the meager stage of Shakespeare's day put a heavy burden upon Shakespeare's audiences which they were able to endure only by heroic efforts of the imagination. The implication is that an Elizabethan audience did its best to dream itself into a Reinhardt setting and that only in so far as it succeeded was the play successful. With all fitting modesty, I doubt it. I doubt whether the bare stage was a disadvantage. I doubt whether it was a disadvantage to have actors by their soliloquies admit that they were actors. The satisfaction of poetry, the satisfaction of all art, comes from the recognition of the poem as a poem, of the work of art as a work of art, and not at all from a muzzy confusion of either with what is so lifelessly called real life. It is conceivable that such non-audiences as that at the opening of *The Cradle Will Rock* might become fairly common if the faked realism of the modern stage could be replaced by the honest realism of a poetic theatre.

PREFACE

by ORSON WELLES

I started producing Marc Blitzstein's music drama the minute it was written almost two years ago, and I have been producing it almost incessantly ever since.

It is unnecessary to review the fabulous stage history of *The Cradle Will Rock*. It is enough to say that it has survived, untarnished, as many proposed and supposed productions as I would like to remember, particularly as they were all mine.

I have produced it in different theatres here in the metropolitan district, and out in the steel towns, with different casts and in different ways. I have produced it with and without benefit of orchestra, on illuminated glass wagons, and even in the audience, with and without the audience.

I have produced it entirely without two separate and distinct scenic designers and with and without permission of four theatrical managements, including our own United States Government.

This makes me undisputed world authority on producing *The Cradle Will Rock*.

I put this claim in print because and not in spite of the significant circumstance that *The Cradle Will Rock* in its second Broadway run is enjoying its most brilliant success in the entire absence of any production whatsoever.

The work is apparently indestructible. And what is more interesting, it is certainly entirely new.

The arts of Music and the Play have had efficient business relationships in the past, an occasional partnership and a few happy marriages. Here, finally, is their first off-spring. It is a love-child, and besides being legitimate, it looks like both its parents, and it is called a "music drama."

As a matter of fact, it isn't easy to find a title for a new art form.

Just now of course this one has only one real name: *The Cradle Will Rock*.

January 10, 1938

The action takes place in Steeltown, U. S. A., on the night of a union drive.

SCENE 1. Streetcorner
SCENE 2. Nightcourt
SCENE 3. Mission
SCENE 4. Lawn of Mr. Mister's home
SCENE 5. Drugstore
SCENE 6. Hotellobby
SCENE 7. Nightcourt
SCENE 8. Facultyroom
SCENE 9. Dr. Specialist's Office
SCENE 10. Nightcourt

The Cradle Will Rock was produced by the Mercury Theatre, New York, on Sunday night, December 5, 1937. It was staged by Orson Welles with the following cast:

MOLL	Olive Stanton
GENT	George Fairchild
DICK	Guido Alexander
COP	Robert Farnsworth
REVEREND SALVATION	Hiram Sherman
EDITOR DAILY	Bert Weston
YASHA	Edward Fuller
DAUBER	John Hoysradt
PRESIDENT PREXY	Hansford Wilson
PROFESSOR TRIXIE	George Smithfield
DR. SPECIALIST	Frank Marvel
HARRY DRUGGIST	John Adair
MR. MISTER	Will Geer
MRS. MISTER	Peggy Coudray
JUNIOR MISTER	Hiram Sherman
SISTER MISTER	Dulce Fox
STEVE	Howard Bird
BUGS	Geoffrey Powers
SADIE POLOCK	Marian Rudley
GUS POLOCK	George Fairchild
LARRY FOREMAN	Howard da Silva
PROFESSOR SCOOT	Hiram Sherman
ELLA HAMMER	Blanche Collins
CLERK, REPORTER, PROFESSOR MAMIE	Marc Blitzstein

CHORUS: Helen Carter, Lucille Schly, Robert Clark, Larry Lauria, E. Sidney, Lilia Hallums, Ralph Ramson, Billy Bodkins, Alma Dixon, Abner Dorsey.

STAGE MANAGER: William Herz.

To

BERT BRECHT

THE CRADLE WILL ROCK

SCENE ONE

STREETCORNER

Enter MOLL.

MOLL

  At lamp post.
I'm checkin home now, call it a night.
Goin up to my room, turn on the light—
Jesus, turn off that light.
I ain't in Steeltown long.
I work two days a week;
The other five my efforts ain't required.
For two days out of seven
Two dollar bills I'm given;
So I'm just searchin along the street,
For on those five days it's nice to eat.
Jesus, Jesus, who said let's eat?
  Enter GENT.

GENT

Hello, baby.

MOLL

Hello, big boy.

GENT

Busy, baby?

23

MOLL

Not so very.

GENT

I'd like to give you a hundred bucks,
But I only got thirty cents.

MOLL

Say, would you wait till I catch my breath
On account of it's so immense?
Make it a dollar.

GENT

Honest, kid, nix, that's all I got—thirty cents.

MOLL

Go on, make it eighty.

GENT

Thirty cents.

MOLL

Seventyfive.

GENT

I said thirty.

MOLL

Come on, big boy, don't be that way.
Half a buck?

GENT

Listen, you, I said what I mean—thirty cents—
Get me?

She takes his arm.

What's the idea?—hey, leggo my arm!

MOLL

Listen, big boy, I'll be nice, come on, big boy. . . .

GENT

Leggo my arm—

MOLL

Don't be a sap, come on and . . .

GENT

Yeh. . . .

MOLL

Listen, mister . . .

GENT

I know—lay off. . . .

MOLL

Please . . .

GENT

All the sob stuff . . .

MOLL

Now you know. . . .

GENT

Try to . . .

MOLL

I wouldn't . . .

GENT

Rush me, huh?

25

MOLL

Mister . . .

GENT

Cheese it, a dick!
Enter DICK.

DICK

What's goin on here?

MOLL

Oh, nothin.

DICK

Oh, yeh? Nothin, huh?

GENT

Nothing, officer, nothing at all. We was just talkin.

DICK

Talkin, huh? Heard you a mile away! . . . Masher, huh?

GENT

Certainly not, officer!

DICK

Aw, shut up! Oughta pull you both in.

GENT

Now, look here, officer . . .

26

DICK

Slip us your dough—quick!
    GENT *pulls out bill, hands it over.*
Okay, melt.

GENT

Melt . . . ? Oh, melt. . . .
    Exit.
    MOLL *and* DICK *laugh—she is a bit nervous.*

MOLL

He was kinda annoyin me.

DICK

Yeh?

MOLL

What's the trouble tonight? Where's everybody?

DICK

All down in front of Union Headquarters, I guess.
Big union drive tonight.

MOLL

Gee!

DICK

What do you mean, gee?
Union trouble ain't no news in this burg.
All the force gets called out regular.
Just your luck I happened to be around here now.

27

MOLL

You must be busy.
I bet they need you bad.

DICK

Sure, they need me bad. See that phone over there?
They'll send for me when things begin to pop.

MOLL

Well, good night, officer—good night and thank you.
I think maybe I'll go down and see the fun.

DICK

Hold your horses there!
A little girlie all alone in this gloom?
Why, you need my protection right to your room.
Come on and smile now, sister.

MOLL

Say, you got me wrong!

DICK

Yeh?

MOLL

Why, you're no better than that two-bit clod!
Maybe you're part of the new vice squad . . .

DICK

Howdya guess it, baby?

MOLL

So that's the way you work it, now I see,
A Romeo that's on the make.
Try to throw a little scare in me,
Because I need a break to make a livin!
What the hell do you care what I do
So long as you get what I'm givin?
Ain't it nice knowin that you got me comin and goin?

DICK

Hey, wait a minute,
Say, I don't get you. . .
Whatsa matter with me?

MOLL

Don't get me wrong, I've loved you all along.
Yes, indeed, you're just my style.
All the girls go crazy at your call,
You've got that certain smile that makes em fall,
Come on, you lug, go put me in the jug!
You think you're wise, you think you own me!
I'll show you guys . . .
The phone rings.

DICK

Hello—yeh, Dick talkin. What's up? Square in front
of Union Headquarters? Who phoned in? Virgil? Go
on—eight of em? What are they, strikers? Listenin to
a speech, is that all? You know Virgil—

29

The sound of a quarrel, angry voices.
Wait a minute, here he comes now!

> *Hangs up. Enter* Cop *and* Liberty Committee, *which comprises:* Reverend Salvation—*sleek, urbane, deferential;* Editor Daily—*glib, the cigar-straw-hat kind;* Yasha, *a violinist, and* Dauber, *an artist—the Gold Dust Twins of a provincial art-world;* President Prexy—*timid, thin-lipped;* Professors Mamie *and* Trixie—*one a bit seedy and pompous, the other frankly tough and unacademic, the football coach; finally,* Dr. Specialist—*Steeltown's "big" physician. They are all in a state of considerable excitement.*

Cop
You're all under arrest!

Liberty Committee
Arrest?

Dr. Specialist
But, officer . . .

Reverend Salvation
You can't arrest us. . . .

Dauber
Do we look like Union organizers?

THE CRADLE WILL ROCK

TRIXIE
It was that man!

PREXY
Do we look like steel workers?

TRIXIE
It was that man!

COP
I said, you're under arrest!

DR. SPECIALIST
Why, we were sent by Mr. Mister!

REVEREND SALVATION
Yes, Mr. Mister!

EDITOR DAILY
You can't do this to us! Why, Mr. Mister sent us!

TRIXIE
It was that man!

YASHA
That man who was making the speech!

DAUBER
It was him you were supposed to arrest!

COP
Then what'd you wanna run for?

31

DICK

So, this is the crew.

LIBERTY COMMITTEE

Crew—what a word!

COP

Yes—nice job, huh? Just like that—wasn't out five minutes. Eight of 'em—count 'em. What you got there, Dick?

DICK

Little hustler.

LIBERTY COMMITTEE

Hustler?—tart!

DICK

We can take em all in together.

COP

Suits me—only these are mine.

EDITOR DAILY

Together?

YASHA

Us?

DAUBER

With that?

TRIXIE

With her?

32

REVEREND SALVATION

But you don't know who we are!

DAUBER

You fool!!!

EDITOR DAILY

Idiot!

TRIXIE

Imbecile!

PREXY

Moron!

The LIBERTY COMMITTEE *goes into a small paroxysm.*

COP

Oh, callin me names now!

DAUBER

Go right ahead. You only happen to be arresting the newly-formed Liberty Committee.

COP

Oh, yeh? What's 'at?

EDITOR DAILY

You never heard of the Liberty Committee?

YASHA

A little shriek.

33

DAUBER

Did you ever hear of the Daughters of the American Revolution?

COP

You ain't one of them, are you? Hey, did you say revolution? I knew it! Come on!

General hubbub as the DICK *with the* MOLL *and the* COP *with the* LIBERTY COMMITTEE *go off.*

SCENE TWO

NIGHTCOURT

The scene is empty, except for the CLERK, *busy with papers, and* HARRY DRUGGIST, *who sits alone on the bench.* DRUGGIST *is a derelict; his coat buttoned about his ears, no hat. Traces of a once-comfortable middle-class life stick to him.*

DRUGGIST

Gosh, it's cold in here;
You don't have it heated like
You did last—Thursday?

CLERK

Well, when you get brought in next Thursday,
I'll see you get a cozy fire and a furlined rockingchair.
Would you like that?

DRUGGIST

It's nothing, only I'm a little chilly—
You're kidding me.

CLERK

Sardonic.
No!

35

THE CRADLE WILL ROCK

*Enter with commotion—*DICK *and* MOLL, *followed by* COP *bringing in* REVEREND SALVATION, EDITOR DAILY, YASHA, DAUBER, PRESIDENT PREXY, PROFESSOR MAMIE, PROFESSOR TRIXIE, DR. SPECIALIST. *MOLL *finds a seat next to* DRUGGIST. *The music whips up.*

DAUBER
Hurry up and telephone to Mr. Mister,
To hurry up and come to the rescue!

LIBERTY COMMITTEE
Hurry up and telephone to Mr. Mister
To hurry up and come to the rescue!

EDITOR DAILY
Hurry up and telephone to Mr. Mister
To hurry up and come to the rescue!
Music again.
This is quite an outrage
To be arrested this way!

PROFESSOR MAMIE
This is quite indecent.
They don't know who we are!

LIBERTY COMMITTEE
Phone to Mr. Mister
To come and bail us all out!

36

Cop

Cut out the remarks now, you'll do your talkin later.

Dauber

Think of what my people
Would think if they could see me!

Yasha

Think of what my public
Would think if *they* could see me!

Professor Trixie

You know Mr. Mister.
He'll come and bail us all out.

Liberty Committee

Phone to Mr. Mister
To come and bail us out!
The music simmers down.

Moll

Gee, but they make a lotta noise.
I'm kinda scared.

Druggist

There's nothing to be frightened at.
Tell me, what are you in for?

Moll

Solicitin, I guess.

37

But really because that flatfoot couldn't make me say
   yes.
Say, do you know the others there?
They wouldn't talk to me.
I can see that I ain't in their class.
And say, that goes for you, too.

DRUGGIST

I must admit they're new to
The place, but their faces
Should be seen more often in this place.
Just like mine; I get arrested every week,
Yes, and sometimes twice a week.
Vagrancy it's called—I guess that's me.

MOLL

A crazy life, I'd find it.

DRUGGIST

Well, really I don't mind it, I like the company.
It's lonely looking where my drugstore used to be.
   The music stops.

PREXY

We're the most respectable families in the city!
We're Steeltown's Liberty Committee!

YASHA

We're against the union!
We're against the drive!

THE CRADLE WILL ROCK

DICK

Hey, Virgil, tell me now,
What's it all about tonight?

COP

What I told you at Union Headquarters,
That's about all tonight.
Mr. Mister sent in orders,
Arrest everybody formin a crowd.
A fella started makin a speech—
I pulled in all the guys I could reach.
A chord punctuates it.

PROFESSOR MAMIE

Oh, but we were there to stop the man who was mak-
  ing the speech!
He's a red, one of these agitators!
We wanted you to arrest him!

EDITOR DAILY

Why, I drew up the manifesto:
"Steeltown is clean, Steeltown's a real town;"

LIBERTY COMMITTEE

The barbershop attack.
"We don't want a union in Steeltown!"

YASHA

But the other one was mine:
"America, Cradle of Liberty—
Steeltown, Cradle of the Liberty Committee."

39

Professor Mamie

I'm the secretary.

Dr. Specialist

I'm the chairman, and Mr. Mister's personal doctor!

Dauber

I'm his daughter's art instructor!

Liberty Committee

We're Mr. Mister's Liberty Committee!
Another punctuating chord.

Dick

I hope you ain't made a bad break;
They're a kinda refined-lookin bunch, you know.

Cop

Maybe I made a mistake;
I got my orders, that's all I know.
The quieter music again.

Druggist

That's why they're all in here, then.
The cop got his signals mixed.
Shall I tell you a secret?
We're in the same old trade as you.

Moll

You mean you're all solicitin?

40

THE CRADLE WILL ROCK

DRUGGIST
Not quite, but so to say;
They won't buy our milkwhite bodies,
So we kinda sell out in some other way—
To Mr. Mister.

MOLL
Who is this Mr. Mister?

DRUGGIST
Better ask me who he's not.
He owns steel and everything else too. . . .
Because of him my son
Was killed six months ago. . . .
Now he'll come and bail them out!

MOLL
Say, would he bail us out, too?

DRUGGIST
I don't know, I'm drunk.
The music stops.

REVEREND SALVATION
I wonder if I hadn't better phone Mrs. Mister?
I know her so much better than I know Mr. Mister.

EDITOR DAILY
I'm afraid Mr. Mister's got his hands full tonight.

41

Professor Mamie and Professor Trixie
Will it keep him from coming here? Will it?

Editor Daily
That union business comes to a head tonight—
He's going crazy trying to kill it.

Dauber
Officer, Officer, where's the man who made the speech?
Chords.

Liberty Committee
Yes, where's the man who made the speech?

Prexy
We're in here—

Editor Daily
But where's he?

Liberty Committee
Where's the man who made the speech?
Chords.

Cop
All right, take it easy, we got him, don't get sore,
He'll be here. The boys are givin him a little workout
    next door.
Anybody want to join him?

42

LIBERTY COMMITTEE
Very loud and doleful.
Oh, what a filthy nightcourt!
Place for common tramps and bums.
Don't they know nice people when they see them?
We prosecute defendants; it's not our place to be them!
So, Mr. Mister, please have pity—
Come and save your pet committee from disaster!
Where's the Judge? Where's the Judge?
We want the Judge!

CLERK
Order in the courtroom! Order in the courtroom!
The Judge will be here shortly. In the meantime I'll
    take down the names.
First case: name?

REVEREND SALVATION
Smooth as treacle.
I am Reverend Salvation; I wear the holy cloth. My
name is known to all Godfearing people in Steeltown.
The Liberty Committee has been formed by us to com-
bat socialism, communism, radicalism, and especially
unionism, and to uphold the Constitution—

CLERK
All right, all right; charge?

43

Cop

Well, I had orders—loiterin, I guess—or maybe obstructin traffic. . . .

Reverend Salvation

This is preposterous; the officer has made a dreadful mistake! I insist that everything be placed in the record.

Druggist

So they got old man Salvation in the nightcourt at last. Do you know what the charge ought to be? "Habitual prostitute since 1915."

SCENE THREE

MISSION

1915. Mrs. Mister *and* Reverend Salvation.

Reverend Salvation

My dear Mrs. Mister!

Mrs. Mister

*She is chairman of all the women's clubs in
Steeltown. She has dreamed of Poiret, Rumpel-
mayer's, even Lucius Beebe. Back in 1915 she
was already a salad, with accent on the dressing.*
Reverend Salvation, how are you?
It's been weeks I wanted to meet you and to greet you:
I'm a stray lamb, too.
And I've brought along our monthly present.
Hands him envelope.
But one thing's not so pleasant,
Father dear; I fear
That things cannot continue forever. . . .

Hard times, I can assure you;
Hard times, poor us and poor you;·
Hard times, Father; what can we do?

45

THE CRADLE WILL ROCK

The market hasn't been ideal:
We have to sell our steel
To French or English or German,
Though the latter are vermin.
Father, please, in your sermon Sunday—
I rely upon you to implore that *we* stay out of the war!

REVEREND SALVATION
Mounts pulpit.
Thou shalt not kill. . . .
So saith it in the Bible. So must it be.
A chorale.

Thou shalt not kill.
Peace on earth, towards men good will—
Nothing but good will.
As your shepherd, I implore,
Turn from thoughts of wicked war,
War we do abhor.

Women, save your husbands, sons and sweethearts!
Men, be resolute, refuse, refuse to shoot!
Or into the loathsome fray we'll be tossed.
Everything be lost: Oh, peace at any cost!

CHORUS
Which is to say everybody.
Amen.

46

THE CRADLE WILL ROCK

REVEREND SALVATION

Brightly.
Collection!

DRUGGIST'S VOICE

. . . The next year, 1916—
SALVATION *steps off pulpit.*

MRS. MISTER

*She has changed her hat, to something
pretty awful and 1916.*
Reverend Salvation, I'm worried.
Things are not proceeding so nicely,
Or precisely in the way they should.
And my husband, Mr. Mister, said it's
Something about bank credits.
Father, dear, they fear
For steel, and oil—and rubber!

So we must set the town right.
Hands him envelope.
Please don't be quite so downright.
Simply answer both yes and no.
It's true you've preached so much for peace—
But now it seems that peace may be a little expensive;
Please don't think me offensive!
Just restrain your intensive ardor.
You might mention that you do deplore
The *German* side of the war!

47

REVEREND SALVATION

Mounts pulpit.

Thou shalt not—um.

Clears his throat importantly. The chorale has a variation.

Righteousness conquers, iniquity perishes,
Peace is a wonderful thing!
But when I say peace, I'm referring to *inner* peace,
Let there be no misconception!
The peace, you remember, which passeth beyond
    understanding.
We must remember our honor,
And the valor and pride which is ours to cherish and
    use.
Knowing well that peace without honor
No good American should excuse!
Surely I need not remind you
Of the war which is simply dreadful for everyone.
There we take no sides, still we know
Who defends sweet peace from the savage Hun!

CHORUS

Amen.

REVEREND SALVATION

Collection!

DRUGGIST'S VOICE

. . . But, in 1917—

48

THE CRADLE WILL ROCK

MRS. MISTER

*A new hat, all plumes—now she is violent, a
harridan.*

Reverend Salvation! News!
Front-page news! Headline news!
Strictly, mind, confidential news!
But such news! Ha!
My-husband's-just-got-back-from-a-conference,
And-he-says-it's-the-only-way-to-recoup-our-profits,
It's-all-fixed-and-everything's-ready-for-the-first-guns!

WAR! WAR! Kill all the dirty Huns!
WAR! WAR! Kill all the dirty Huns!
WAR! WAR! We're entering the war!
For Mr. Mister's shown the President how things are—
England has simply been a darling!
Eyes right! Think of the rallies!
Eyes left! I'm going to knit socks!
Eyes front! Steel's going to go up skyhigh!
All you clergymen must now prepare a special prayer
And do your share! Oh, yes—your share . . .
Hands him envelope.

REVEREND SALVATION

Mounts pulpit.
Thou—shalt—

BOTH (*and chorus*)

WAR! WAR! Kill all the dirty Huns!
And those Austrungarians!

WAR! WAR! We're entering the war!
The *Lusitania's* an unpaid debt,
Remember Troy! Remember Lafayette!
Remember the Alamo! Remember our womanhood!
Remember those innocent unborn babies!

MRS. MISTER

Don't let George do it, you do it!

EVERYBODY

Make the world safe for Democracy!
Make the world safe for Liberty!
Make the world safe for Steel and the Mister family!

REVEREND SALVATION

The chorale.
Of course, it's peace we're for—
This is war to end all war!

CHORUS

Amen.

MRS. MISTER

I can see the market rising like a beautiful bird!

REVEREND SALVATION

Collection!

FLASHBACK TO NIGHTCOURT

CLERK

Order in the courtroom! Order in the courtroom!
Next case: Name?

EDITOR DAILY

I am Editor Daily of the Steeltown *News.*

CLERK

Charge?

COP

The same I guess; you know about these things—
What *have* I got these people for? Loiterin?
Obstructin traffic?

DRUGGIST

Change that to read "Procurer, also known as pimp"—
To Mr. Mister—to Sister Mister—to Junior Mister—

SCENE FOUR

LAWN OF MR. MISTER'S HOME

JUNIOR *and* SISTER MISTER *enter in gliding hammocks.*
JUNIOR *is sluggish, collegiate and vacant;* SISTER *is smartly
gotten-up and peevish.*

SISTER

Junior!

JUNIOR

Leave me alone.

SISTER

You big lump! Why don't you try to reduce?

JUNIOR

Don't bother me, I'm busy.
He warbles; his hammock swings.
Croon, croon till it hurts, baby,
Croon, my heart asserts, baby,
Croonin in spurts, baby,
Is just the nerts for a tune!

SISTER

Her hammock swings; it's her turn.
Spoon, in a canoe, baby!
Spoon, one built for two, baby,

CROON SPOON

Words and Music by Marc Blitzstein

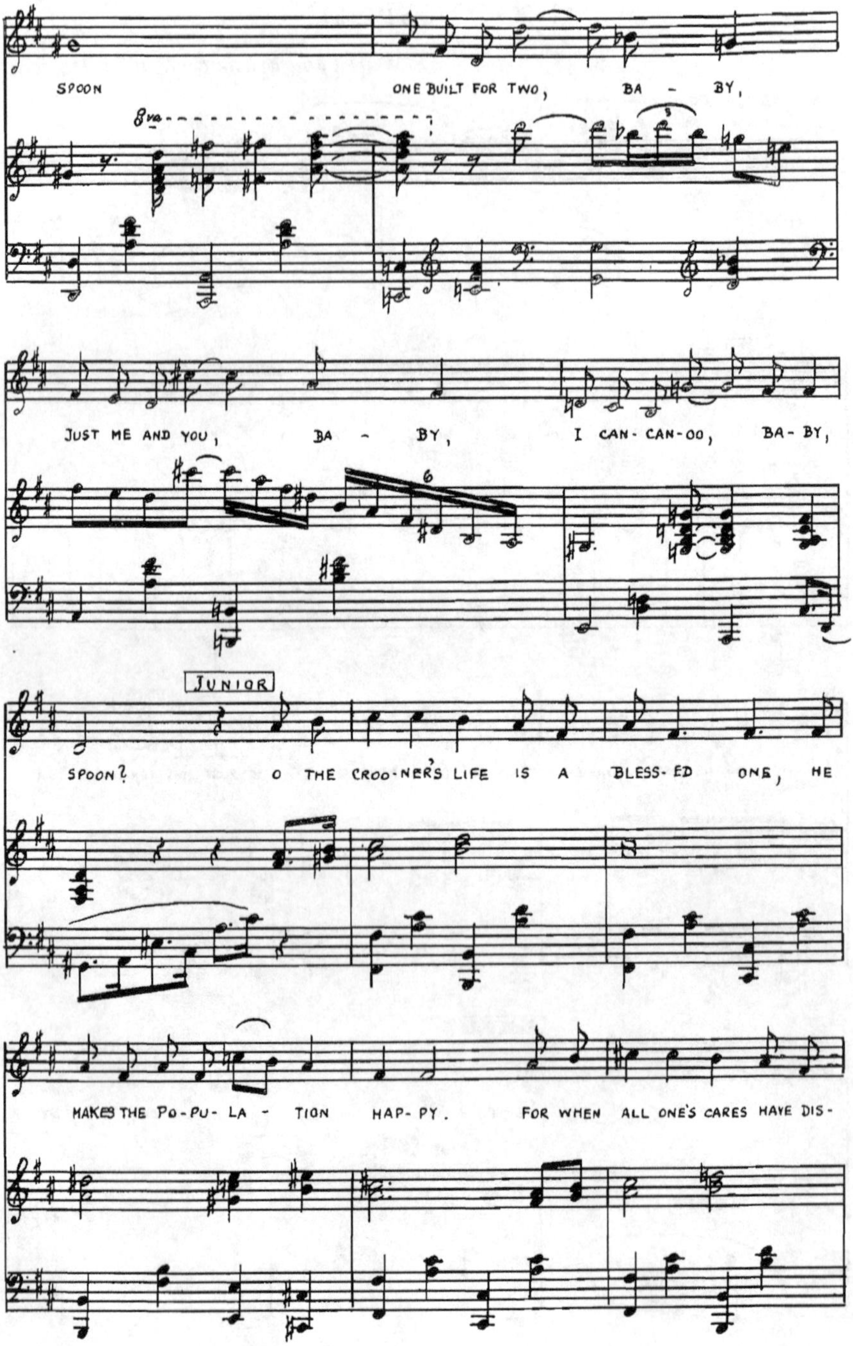
SPOON ONE BUILT FOR TWO, BA - BY,
8va
JUST ME AND YOU, BA - BY, I CAN-CAN-OO, BA-BY,
JUNIOR
SPOON? O THE CROO-NER'S LIFE IS A BLESS-ED ONE, HE
MAKES THE PO-PU-LA - TION HAP-PY. FOR WHEN ALL ONE'S CARES HAVE DIS-

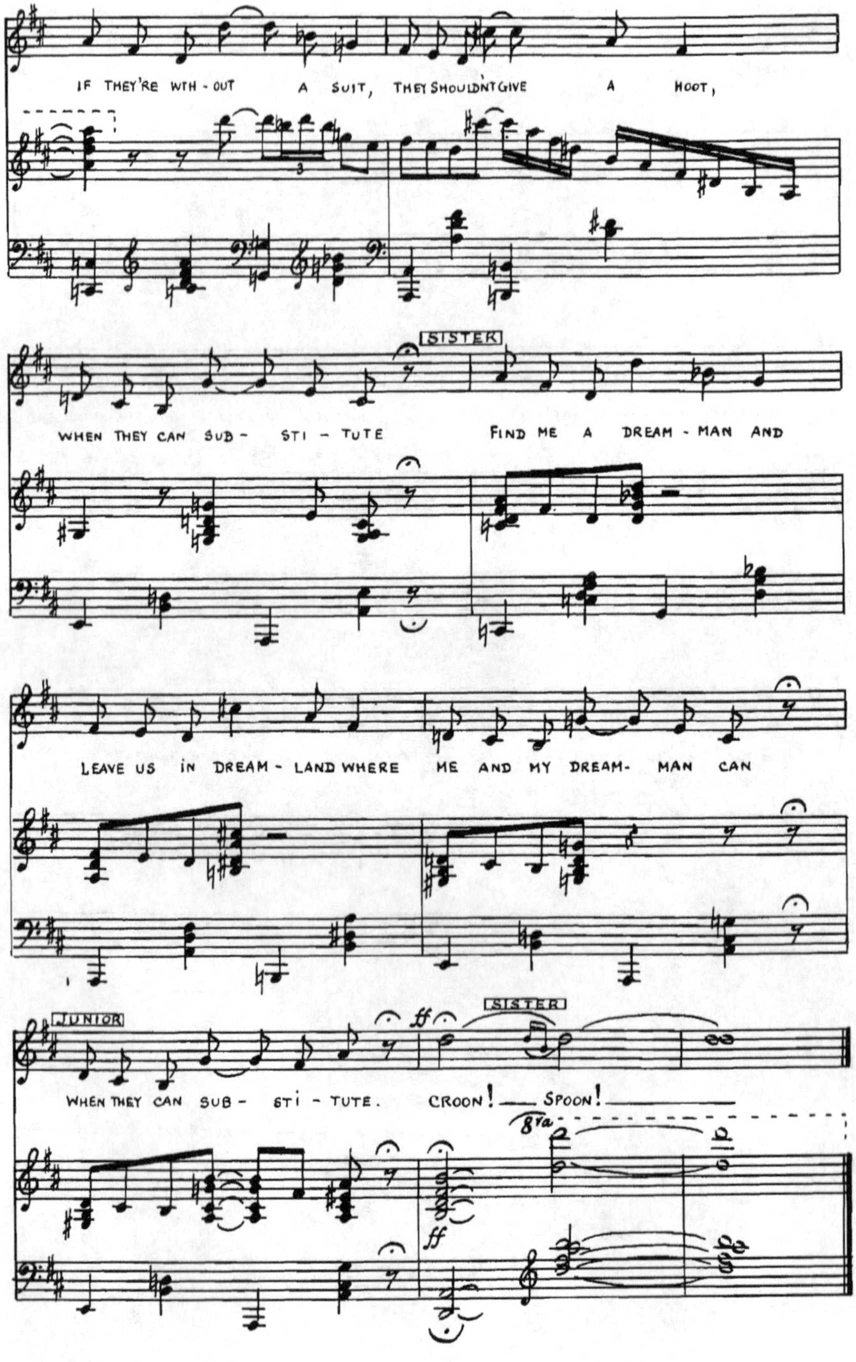
IF THEY'RE WITH - OUT A SUIT, THEY SHOULDN'T GIVE A HOOT,
SISTER
WHEN THEY CAN SUB - STI - TUTE FIND ME A DREAM - MAN AND
LEAVE US IN DREAM - LAND WHERE ME AND MY DREAM - MAN CAN
JUNIOR
SISTER
WHEN THEY CAN SUB - STI - TUTE. CROON! SPOON!
ff
8va

THE CRADLE WILL ROCK

Just me and you, baby,
I can,—can-oo, baby, spoon?

JUNIOR
He practically bellows.
Oh, the crooner's life is a blessèd one,
He makes the population happy.
For when all one's cares have distressèd one—

SISTER
She can still top him.
Oh, to spoon is grand in the Juneday sun,
You spoon and spoon and never get tired!
But it's nicer at night than in the noonday sun—
Cause then you're Gary Cooper and I'm Carole
    Lombard!

JUNIOR
Just croon! even the poor are not immune.
If they're without a suit,
They shouldn't give a hoot,
When they can substitute—

SISTER
Find me a Dream-man and
Leave us in Dreamland
Where me and my Dream-man can—

JUNIOR

When they can substitute—CROON!

SISTER

SPOON!
Enter MR. MISTER *and* EDITOR DAILY.

MR. MISTER

Do we disturb you two unduly?
I have business with Editor Daily.

JUNIOR

Should I wear stripes or checks?
Oh, the problems of my attire!
Scuse me, I got to make another long distance call
    to *Esquire*.

SISTER

And I got a date—with a fig! Get it?
    They exit.

MR. MISTER

He is so much the archetype of all the MR.
*MISTERS in the world that he resembles the
type not at all; is, in fact, rather eccentric, a
distinct individual.*
The children are rather witty. . . .
I have called you here fairly early,
My dear Editor Daily,
Because I have something on my mind.

58

THE CRADLE WILL ROCK

EDITOR DAILY

All my gift at prose'll
Be at your disposal,
Mr. Mister, you've been very kind.

MR. MISTER

I believe newspapers
Are great mental shapers;
My steel industry is dependent on them really.

EDITOR DAILY

Just you call the *News,*
And we'll tell all the news,
From coast to coast, and from border to border.

MR. MISTER

Yes, but some news—can be made to order.

BOTH

Oh, the press, the press, the freedom of the press!
They'll never take away the freedom of the press!
We must be free to say whatever's on our chest—
With a hey-diddle-dee and a ho-nonny-no
For whichever side will pay the best.

MR. MISTER

I should like a series on young Larry Foreman.
Who goes around stormin and organizin unions.

59

THE CRADLE WILL ROCK

EDITOR DAILY
Yes, we've heard of him,
In fact, good word of him;
He seems quite popular with workingmen.

MR. MISTER
Find out who he drinks with and talks with and sleeps
    with,
And look up his past till at last you've got it on him.

EDITOR DAILY
But the man's so full of fight, he's simply dynamite,
Why, it would take an army to tame him.

MR. MISTER
Then it shouldn't be too hard to frame him.

BOTH
Oh, the press, the press, the freedom of the press!
You've only got to hint whatever's fit to print;
If something's wrong with it, why, then we'll print
    to fit.
With a hey-diddle-dee and a ho-nonny-no
For whichever side will pay the best.

MR. MISTER
Have his picture fill the front page of your paper.
This drunkard and raper who's out to gull the people.

60

THE CRADLE WILL ROCK

EDITOR DAILY

Just a minute, I'm not being indiscreet!
I must consult the owner of my sheet.

MR. MISTER

Please don't try to cross your good-humored new boss—
I'm the owner of your famous paper since this morn-
    ing.

EDITOR DAILY

In that case, I wonder if my place
Is not worth more? The other crowd
Would like me to shake you.

MR. MISTER

Then you'll see just how neatly I'll break you.

BOTH

Oh, the press, the press, the freedom of the press!
They'll never take away the freedom of the press!

MR. MISTER

That Foreman series now?

EDITOR DAILY

Yes, Mr. Mister, yes!

BOTH

With a hey-diddle-dee
And a ho-nonny-no—
    EDITOR DAILY, *a tenor, prolongs the last "no."*

61

MR. MISTER

No?

EDITOR DAILY

Yes, sir! Yes! Yes!

BOTH

For whichever side will pay the best!
The tune is over.

EDITOR DAILY

I agree with you absolutely, Mr. Mister.

MR. MISTER

Now, that's a big relief, Editor Daily.

EDITOR DAILY

You see, I was literary adviser for years
To Princess Wallawallahuanee—of the Hawaiian
Islands!
We still correspond.

MR. MISTER

Then you're just the man to write the manifesto
For my new Liberty Committee.

EDITOR DAILY

If I do say so myself—

MR. MISTER

A literary adviser to a Princess, what do you know!

THE CRADLE WILL ROCK

EDITOR DAILY

Yes, well, spelling and things—you know.
JUNIOR *is heard whooping it up.*

MR. MISTER

Oh, yes, about Junior . . .

EDITOR DAILY

I do like Junior!

MR. MISTER

He doesn't go so well with union trouble.
I want him out of town, say on the paper;
A correspondent's job or something—see?

EDITOR DAILY

Gulps.
Your Junior—working? Yes, I see!
Enter JUNIOR *and* SISTER, *displaying that other
aspect of boredom—they're going crazy.*

JUNIOR AND SISTER

Let's do something!
So unconventional,
And so intentional
People all around get pale!
Let's do something!

SISTER

Before we've got too old—

THE CRADLE WILL ROCK

Junior

I'm glad I'm not too old
To tie a can to a doggie's tail!

Both

Let's raise chickens,
Raise the dickens,
Go to church and be on time;
For excitement, an indictment
Would be swell if we invent a crime—
But let's do something!
To kill the monotony, let's go in for botany,
If they've got any, and if not any, then
LET'S DO SOMETHING!

Editor Daily

Have you thought of Honolulu
Where your boredom would be banned?
Bid your family toodle-oo-loo,
Sail away to that fair land!
That's just the isle for you—
And you'll have your work, too.
    Junior *is startled.*
A little scribbling on your father's journal.
Oh, nothing ever happens over there!

Mr. Mister

Son, they say the climate's fresh and vernal.

HONOLULU

Words and Music by Marc Blitzstein

Andante
ED
mf
HAVE YOU THOUGHT OF HO-NO - LU - LU? WHERE YOUR BORE-DOM WOULD BE
BANNED? BID YOUR FA-MI-LY TOODLE-OO-LOO. SAIL A-WAY TO THAT FAIR
LAND. THAT'S JUST THE ISLE FOR YOU, AND YOU'LL HAVE
YOUR WORK TOO A LIT-TLE SCRIBB-LING ON YOUR FATH-ER'S JOUR-NAL O,
f

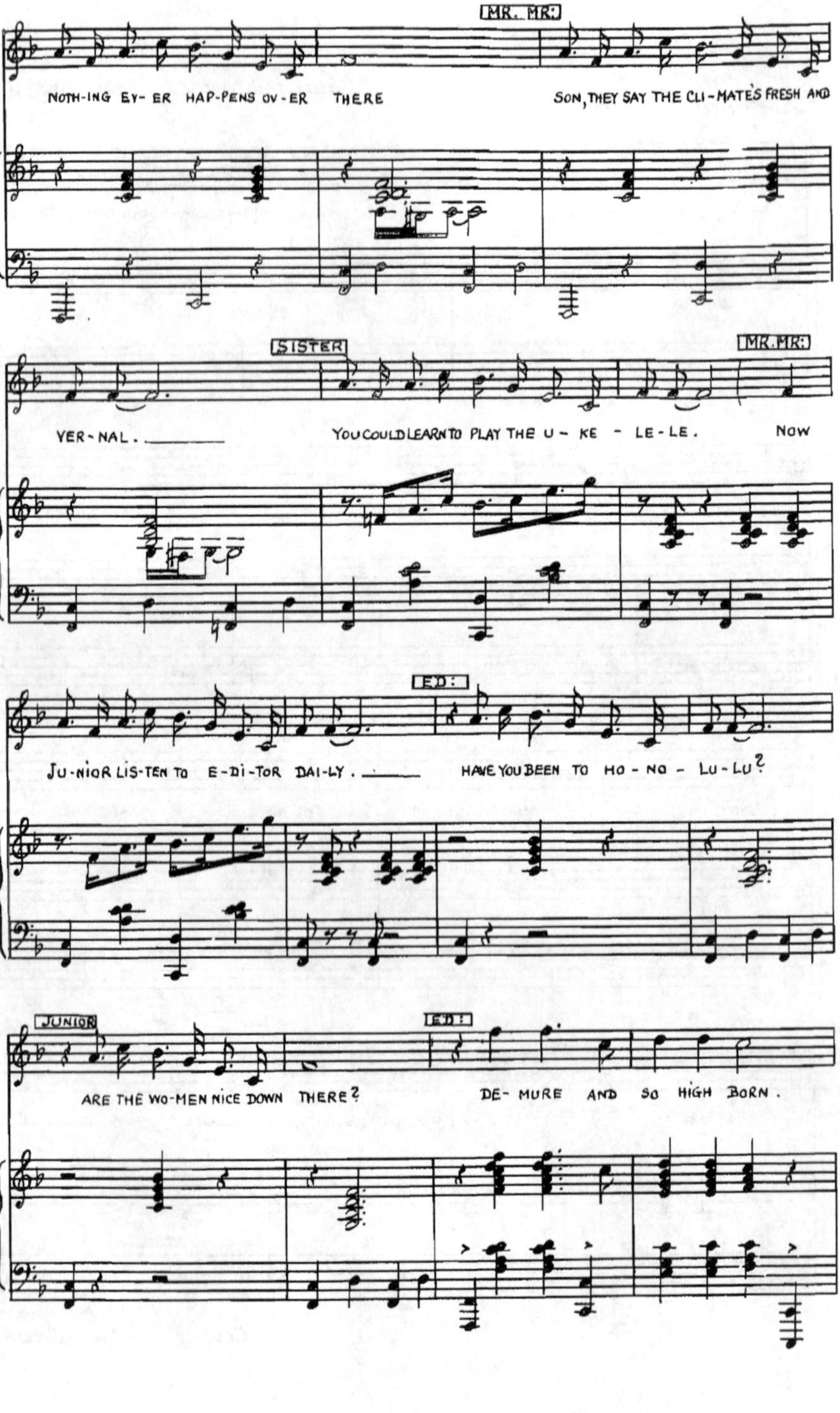

MR. MR:
NOTH-ING EV-ER HAP-PENS OV-ER THERE
SON, THEY SAY THE CLI-MATE'S FRESH AND
SISTER
MR. MR:
VER-NAL.
YOU COULD LEARN TO PLAY THE U-KE-LE-LE.
NOW
ED:
JU-NIOR LIS-TEN TO E-DI-TOR DAI-LY.
HAVE YOU BEEN TO HO-NO-LU-LU?
JUNIOR
ED:
ARE THE WO-MEN NICE DOWN THERE?
DE-MURE AND SO HIGH BORN.

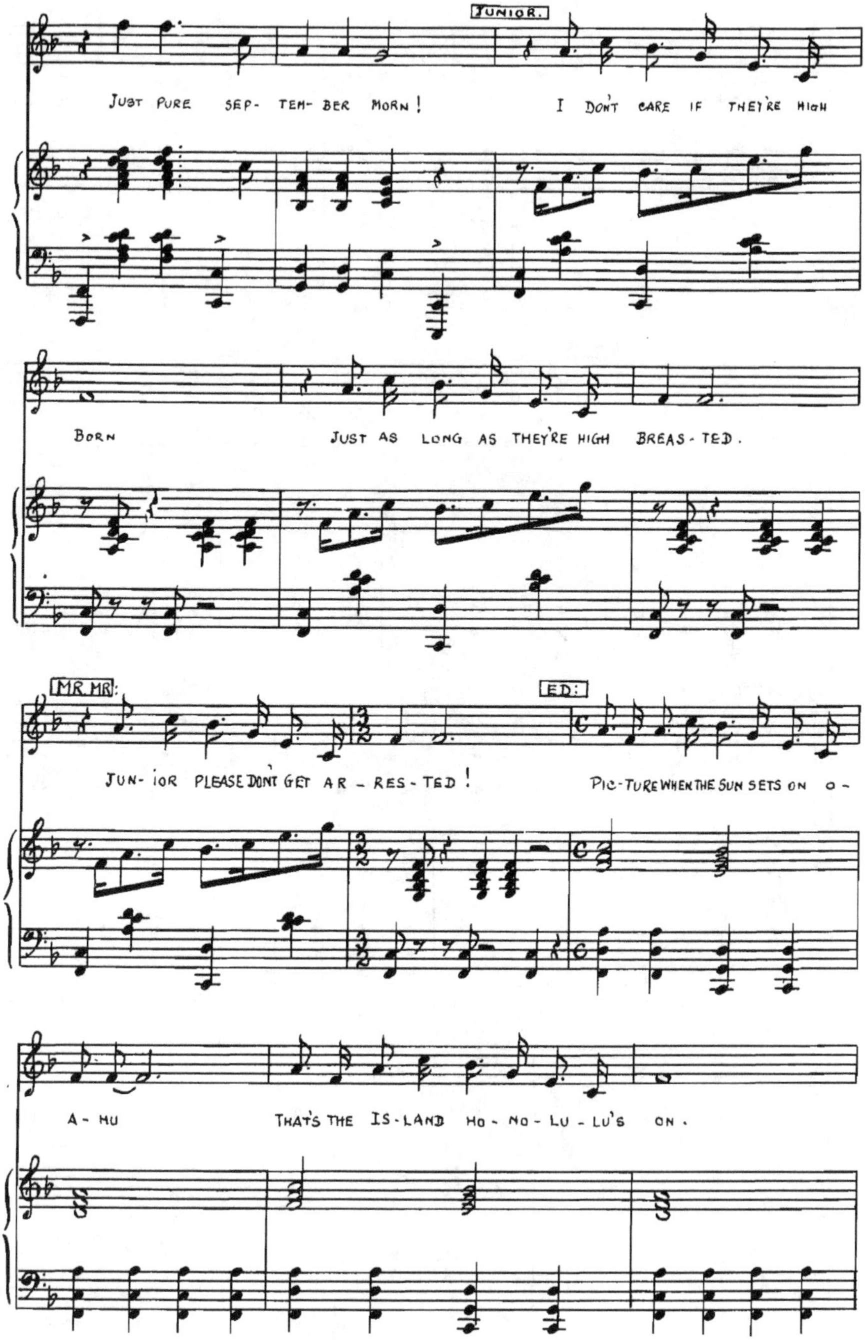
JUNIOR.
JUST PURE SEP- TEM- BER MORN!
I DON'T CARE IF THEY'RE HIGH
BORN
JUST AS LONG AS THEY'RE HIGH BREAS- TED.
MR. MR:
JUN- IOR PLEASE DON'T GET AR - RES - TED!
ED:
PIC- TURE WHEN THE SUN SETS ON O-
A - HU
THAT'S THE IS - LAND HO - NO - LU - LU'S ON.

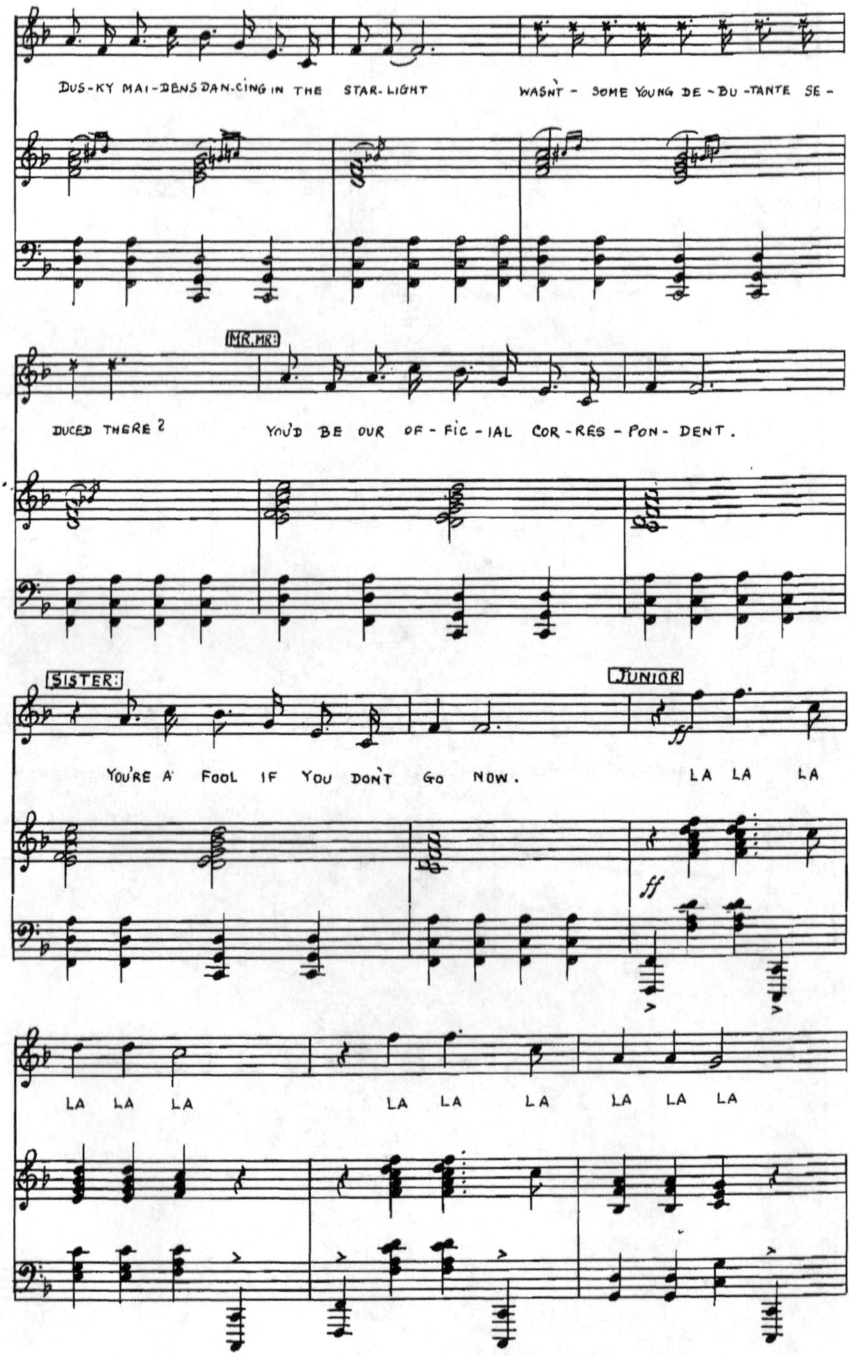
DUS-KY MAI-DENS DAN-CING IN THE STAR-LIGHT WASN'T - SOME YOUNG DE-BU-TANTE SE-
DUCED THERE?
MR. MR:
YOU'D BE OUR OF-FI-CIAL COR-RES-PON-DENT.
SISTER:
YOU'RE A FOOL IF YOU DON'T GO NOW.
JUNIOR
ff
LA LA LA
LA LA LA
LA LA LA
LA LA LA

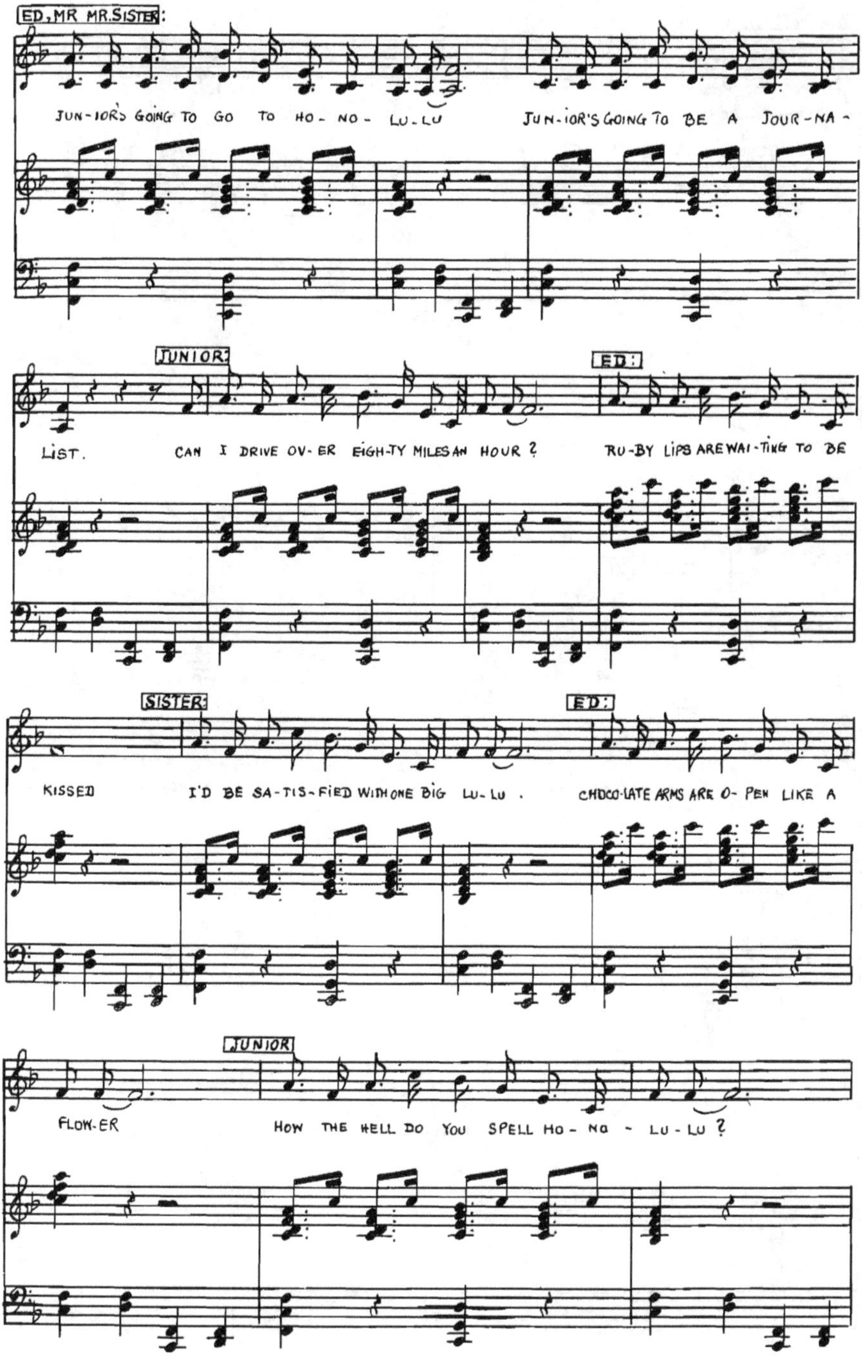
ED, MR MR. SISTER:
JUN-IOR'S GOING TO GO TO HO-NO-LU-LU JUN-IOR'S GOING TO BE A JOUR-NA-LIST.
JUNIOR:
CAN I DRIVE OV-ER EIGH-TY MILES AN HOUR?
ED:
RU-BY LIPS ARE WAI-TING TO BE KISSED
SISTER:
I'D BE SA-TIS-FIED WITH ONE BIG LU-LU.
ED:
CHOCO-LATE ARMS ARE O-PEN LIKE A FLOW-ER
JUNIOR
HOW THE HELL DO YOU SPELL HO-NO-LU-LU?

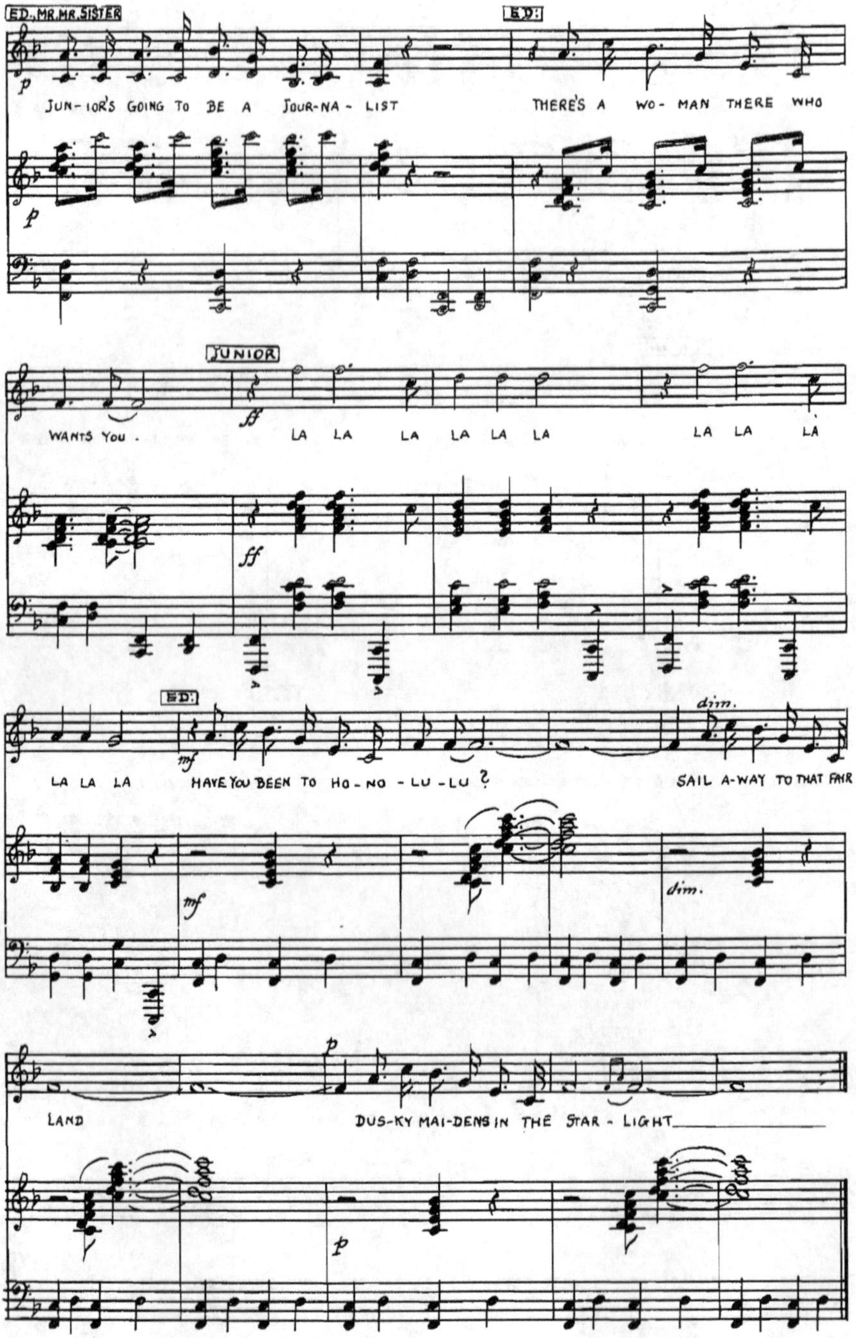
ED., MR., MR., SISTER
JUN-IOR'S GOING TO BE A JOUR-NA-LIST
ED:
THERE'S A WO-MAN THERE WHO WANTS YOU.
JUNIOR
LA LA LA LA LA LA LA LA LA LA LA LA
ED:
HAVE YOU BEEN TO HO-NO-LU-LU?
SAIL A-WAY TO THAT FAIR LAND
DUS-KY MAI-DENS IN THE STAR-LIGHT

SISTER
You could learn to play the ukelele.

MR. MISTER
Now, Junior, listen to Editor Daily.

EDITOR DAILY
Have you been to Honolulu?

JUNIOR
Up to this point perfectly sodden.
Are the women nice down there?

EDITOR DAILY
Ever-ready.
Demure, and so high born,
Just pure September Morn.

JUNIOR
I don't care if they're high born
Just as long as they're highbreasted.

MR. MISTER
Junior, please don't get arrested!

EDITOR DAILY
Picture when the sun sets in Oahu;

71

JUNIOR *is blank.*
That's the island Honolulu's on;
Dusky maidens dancing in the starlight—

SISTER
Wasn't some young debutante seduced there?

MR. MISTER
You'd be our official correspondent.

SISTER
Almost tenderly.
You're a fool if you don't go now.

JUNIOR
*Fortissimo; the moonface bursts into radiance
without warning.*
La la la-la-la la.
La la la-la-la la.

EDITOR DAILY, MR. MISTER, SISTER
In harmony; triumphantly.
Junior's going to go to Honolulu!
Junior's going to be a journalist!

JUNIOR
Can I drive over eighty miles an hour?

EDITOR DAILY
Undaunted.
Ruby lips are waiting to be kissed!

72

THE CRADLE WILL ROCK

SISTER

Not much on geography, but with the right idea.
I'd be satisfied with one big Zulu.

EDITOR DAILY

Chocolate arms are open like a flower.

JUNIOR

Dreamy.
How the hell do you spell Honolulu?

EDITOR DAILY, MR. MISTER, SISTER

They whisper it, not disturbing the dream.
Junior's going to be a journalist!

EDITOR DAILY

There's a woman there who wants you. . . .

JUNIOR

*Fortissimo and sudden again; the baby is given
the rattle.*
La la la-la-la la.
La la la-la-la la.

EDITOR DAILY

Have you been to Honolulu?
Sail away to that fair land . . .
Dusky maidens in the starlight. . . .

Fadeout

FLASHBACK TO NIGHTCOURT

CLERK

Order in the courtroom! Next case: name?

HARRY DRUGGIST

Harry Druggist.

CLERK

Usual charge, I suppose?

COP

You know this one. I picked him up in the square, earlier in the evening.

HARRY DRUGGIST

Wait a minute. I belong with these people. I sold out too—I sold out my boy; and two others with him.

74

SCENE FIVE

DRUGSTORE

DRUGGIST; *and* STEVE, *behind fountain.* DRUGGIST *is a sunny little man, somewhat vague. He bustles about his drugstore with a pleasant sense of importance.* STEVE, *his son, is an agreeable adolescent, really much smarter than his father, and a little amused by him.*

DRUGGIST

Steve!

STEVE

Yes, Pop?

DRUGGIST

Those glasses—really clean this time. Hah—
      Blows on his hand.
Like that!

STEVE

      Tries it with a glass.
Hah?

DRUGGIST

That's the way. . . .
      He sings a bit.
   It looks like summer weather,
   There's a fine warm sun.

75

I swear I'd not change places
With King Solomon.
I ought to make you pay for every glass that you
  drop.
It certainly feels fine to own my shop.

STEVE

Oh, Pop, you're such a crazy;
This shop's not yours; what about the mortgage?

DRUGGIST

The mortgage now!
You know how much it worries me.
I saw the man again, told him to let me be.
I'll pay him when I can.
You know who owns the company?
It's Mr. Mister. Tell me,
What does he want with my little cash?
    He stops singing.
It's a terrible world, Stevie—
And I feel fine.
    He hums.
Da da dee da da da-dum, dee-dee da da da.
    Enter BUGS. BUGS *is an underworld character,*
    one step above the common thug; slicker and
    more presentable.
Are you the guy who runs this joint?

DRUGGIST

I'm the proprietor.

76

BUGS

Do you know a Polock who comes in here every Sunday?

DRUGGIST

A Polock?

BUGS

Sure, a punk. With his wife he comes here.

STEVE

You know, Pop, he means that Polish fellow.

DRUGGIST

Nodding; he remembers.

He brings his wife here every week about this time.
She likes my icecream sodas. Yes, I know them well.

BUGS

You know what he looks like, huh?

DRUGGIST

Yes, why?

BUGS

Uh, you'd like to keep this drugstore, wouldn't you?
You wouldn't want any company to clamp down on
your mortgage or anything like that now, would you?

DRUGGIST

He stares.

What's the idea?

77

BUGS

Here's the dope: When this Polock comes in today,
you don't say nothin. He goes out. There's a big noise
outside. You don't say nothin—nothin, understand? You
keep your trap shut. But when they ast you later on, who
done it-- You remember it's this here Polock.

DRUGGIST

Done—what?

BUGS

Explosion. They're takin a little piece off Union Headquarters acrost the street.

DRUGGIST

A growing alarm on his face.
Who is?

BUGS

None of your damn business. Jeez, I don't know why
the boss hadda pick you outa all the stores on this side!
Talk about dumb!

STEVE

The boss? Mr. Mister's behind this somewhere, Pop!

BUGS

You don't know that name! You never heard that
name before—get me?

78

DRUGGIST

But, man, I can't say somebody did something if he
didn't! Suppose he denies it?

BUGS

Patient.
Listen; I'll go over it all again.
There's gonna be an explosion.
This guy's gonna be *in* the explosion.
He ain't gonna bother you none after that.

DRUGGIST

At last he gets it; tense and quiet.
And his wife, too?

BUGS

Can I help it if his wife never lets him outa her sight?

STEVE

*He has realized all along what is up; now he
leaps forward.*
Pop, I heard what he said—
Pop, you're not going to let him get away with it!

BUGS

Grabs STEVE.
You keep your shirt on.
You don't wanna interfere with yer old man!

79

DRUGGIST

In a panic.
Steve, they got me cornered—I'll lose the store—
They can do it—I'll lose everything!
They got me, Stevie! What shall I do?

STEVE

Pop!

BUGS

Shut up, now! Here they come.
> He holds STEVE *frozen, his hand pressing against an unseen revolver. Enter* GUS *and* SADIE PO-
> LOCK. *They are simple, nice people, just married, terribly in love.* SADIE *is fat, and* GUS *loves her that way. He talks with an accent, but* SADIE *doesn't;* GUS *would never have married a girl with an accent.*

GUS

What store you go to get it?

SADIE

Up on High Street.

GUS

Expensive shop, I bet.

SADIE

No, it ain't—and it's the cutest dress!

GUS

Sadie, Sadie, you gotta new dress already. What you wanna, tak all my money?

SADIE

I know, but, Gus . . .

GUS

Is it pretty dress?

SADIE

Oh, Gus, if you could only see me in it!

GUS

Alri'. Maybe they mak me head guy at the mill, and I get plenty money, ha ha ha.
They sit at fountain.
What you tak, same ting?

SADIE

Vanilla icecream soda, with two scoops.

GUS

Me, nutting; aw chust a Cok-Cola; wait, with a shot lemon maybe. . . . The Manager he come to me yesterday, say I keep away from union, I getta good job; then Larry Foreman, union fella, come to me, say, Gus, don't be fool, you belong with us. Look like I very pop'-lar, everybody want me, I dunno.

Sadie, you gonna have kid soon?

SADIE

Gus!!

GUS

I wanna kid, I wanna son! What I care what they hear? Now I got first papers, pretty soon I be real American citizen. The fella say they need men like me; sure, good hands, strong— He say America need men like me. . . . Sadie—I tink maybe— You gettin big already! We gotta buy you new kinda dress soon, huh?

SADIE

Gus, stop it!
The song.

GUS

Why don't my Sadie tell me she gonna have baby?

SADIE

Now, Gus, I ast you twice today, don't talk that way!

GUS

What I care what they hear?

SADIE

Okay, maybe.

GUS

I make a little bed from wood.
So my son sleep good.

GUS AND SADIE LOVE SONG

Words and Music by Marc Blitzstein

NIGHT - TIME THERE NEV - ER WAS SUCH A BOY

AS WE WILL HAVE AND ALL IN THE RIGHT

TIME

GUS: WASSAMATTA, KID?

Both

So my son sleep good. . . .

We wonder if anyone could be
As much in love as we;
We wonder if anyone ever was before.
They couldn't be any more
Than we are.
There never was such a day
Or such a night time.
There never was such a boy
As we will have,
And all in the right time.

> Gus *tries to pay* Steve. *The boy is nerveless,
> transfixed,* Bugs *still covering him.*

Gus

Whassamatta, kid?

> *He leaves the money on the counter.* Gus *and*
> Sadie *go out.*

Bugs

> *Makes a warning sound. Goes to window, makes
> a sign with his arm to someone across the street.*

Steve

> *Galvanized into action.*

No, wait!

> *He runs out after* Gus *and* Sadie.

85

DRUGGIST

Steve!

STEVE

Running.
Wait, they're gonna get you!

DRUGGIST

Stevie!

The sound of an explosion outside. DRUGGIST
covers his face with his hands. The reverbera-
tion scarcely dies, when . .

SCENE SIX

HOTELLOBBY

YASHA *and* DAUBER *enter from either side, practically stomping. Music furious and gay, settles to a vaudeville vamp-till-ready.*

YASHA

Well, if it isn't my old friend Dauber, the artist!

DAUBER

Well, if it isn't my old friend Yasha, the violinist!
Aside.
He has to be here today.

YASHA

Aside.
Of all the people who walk into a hotel lobby, I meet
him.

DAUBER

How's the concert business?

YASHA

Fine; how's the painting business? I had thirty con-
certs last year.

87

DAUBER

Last year, I sold twelve pictures last year. How about
this year?

YASHA

This year I rely on my talent.

DAUBER

Prospects are lousy for me too. . . .
A patter song.
Don't let me keep you, please be on your way.
You must have many things to do.

YASHA

No, not at all, an appointment today
Brings me to these parts.

DAUBER

Me, too!

YASHA

But the person I'm about to meet,
I doubt you could have met her.
The kind that grovels at my feet,
She'd stay there if I let her.
She's fabulously wealthy,
And although that's not the reason,
I think she can be counted on
To subsidize me all next season!

DAUBER
Your lady friend does resemble a lot
Someone, and that's very queer.

YASHA

Indifferent.
So?

DAUBER
Someone who's meeting me here—

YASHA

Interested.
No!

DAUBER
Is her Pierce Arrow light blue?

YASHA

Alarmed.
Yes!

DAUBER
Not Mrs. Mister?

YASHA
Well, yes—Mrs. Mister!

DAUBER
Me, too!

89

BOTH

Oh, there's something so damned low about the rich!
They're fantastic, they're far-fetched, they're just funny.
They've no impulse, no fine feeling, no great itch!

YASHA

What have they got?

DAUBER

What have they got?

BOTH

What have they got? . . . Money.
The vamp again.

DAUBER

Stupid woman, Mrs. Mister!

YASHA

Stupid? What she doesn't know about music
Would put Heifetz back on his feet again!

DAUBER

She asked me to bring El Greco to tea this summer!

YASHA

This summer?
The song.
Oh, so she mentioned this summer to you:
Did she say where she will be?

DAUBER

No, but we both thought that Paris would do.
Or Capri; she calls it Capree.

YASHA

Why, she promised me Bar Harbor,
With an extra house where I—
But of course, if she has other plans,
I've other fish to fry. . . .

DAUBER

Well, dear Lady Duchess desperately
Wants me at her place;
She's had everyone do her three-quarters;
I'm to do full-face.

YASHA

And I just heard from Marchesa Contessa last week:
She was Matilda Magee.

DAUBER

Well?

YASHA

Now she's divorced the Marquis!

DAUBER

Hell, my Lady Duchess loves me!

YASHA

Swell!

DAUBER

But to wed wealth, so I fear,
Would affect my career.

YASHA

I agree!

BOTH

For there's something so damned low about the rich!
It's incredible, the open way they court you.
All these millionaires, I can't tell which is which.

DAUBER

What can they do?

YASHA

What can they do?

BOTH

What can they do? . . . Support you.
    Enter MRS. MISTER. *They trip over each other*
    trying to get to her.

MRS. MISTER

Ah, there you are, you two—and together!
Who says I haven't brought about a union of the arts?
Painting . . . and Music. . . .
Twin flowers . . . from one stem. . . .
The Spirit!

92

Yasha, those horns are perfect. . . . Imagine

    To DAUBER.

he went and had the horns of my Pierce Arrow tuned to
that motif in Beethoven's *Egmont* Overture . . . you
know: ta, ta, ta-ta-ta, ta-ta-ta, yoo hoo! Dauber, I had an
argument with Hallie Vacuum at lunch whether Picasso
has curly hair . . . now don't tell me, I couldn't bear it
if he was bald! The weekend . . . you're both coming
to me for the weekend!

           YASHA AND DAUBER

    Elaborately.

Oh, yes!

    A rumba duet.

    Ask us again and again, Mrs. Mister.
    Ask us again, we love it. . . .
    Please, now and then,
    Do ask us again!
    Whenever it's convenient, we'll come;
    When it's not, we're always lenient,
    Unless you've found some other bum!
    For we love to sit in the lap of your lush
    And lavish display;
    Although it's only from Friday night
    Till Sunday.
    Your guests are disgusting; your food is too heavy;
    We eat and we drink and we belch
    And we're full and we're ill and we're bored. . . .

MRS. MISTER

It is all quite incomprehensible and hilarious to her.

You boys will kill me!

YASHA AND DAUBER

But we live off the fat of the land;
And for service we don't lift a hand.
We're allowed to be rude,
And insulting and lewd—
    They go into close harmony.
So long may you wave, and forever, amen.
If you'll ask us again, again and again,
Oh, please, Mrs. Mister, just ask us again!

MRS. MISTER

Did I tell you about Rupert Scansion?
The poet, you know, he has
Divine eyes and such sensitive hands,
And he told me I was an old soul,
A very old soul. . . .
He was alluding to my spirit . . .
And he's coming to dinner tonight.

YASHA

    This is serious!
To dinner!

94

DAUBER

Willing to unite against a common enemy.
Cora, you're falling!

YASHA

Cora, we're starving! Ask us to dinner too!

DAUBER

Yes, do!

MRS. MISTER

Bland.
You poor boys!
Artists have to eat, that's all
We're good for, we moneyed people.
Just use us, just step all over us,
If it's only for the good of the cause . . .
Oh, speaking of the cause. . . . I want you two
To join my husband's Liberty Committee.
You will, won't you?

DAUBER   YASHA
Put us down,   And how!

MRS. MISTER

But don't you want to know what it's all about?

YASHA   DAUBER
Politics?   Cora, we're artists!

95

THE CRADLE WILL ROCK

YASHA AND DAUBER

And we love Art for Art's sake!
It's smart, for Art's sake,
To part, for Art's sake,
With your heart, for Art's sake,
And your mind, for Art's sake—
Be blind, for Art's sake,
And deaf, for Art's sake,
And dumb, for Art's sake,
Until, for Art's sake,
They kill, for Art's sake
All the Art for Art's sake!

Sound of the "Egmont" motif on limousine horns outside.

MRS. MISTER

There's the car now!
Dauber . . .

She takes his arm.

Yasha . . .

She takes his.

ALL THREE

As they exit to much Beethoven.

Yoo hoo! Yoo hoo! Yoo hoo!

SCENE SEVEN

NIGHTCOURT

The MOLL *sits on the railing. Halflight.*

MOLL

It was Tuesday last week, yeh, Tuesday
I had breakfast at Andy's—
Coffee-and; for lunch
I had coffee-and again;
For dinner I could only afford
Coffee. Then I looked on the floor,
And I see a nickel shinin there. Gee!
    Steps on it.
Coffee-*and,* Andy!
Then I looked closer—
That wasn't no nickel.
Not coffee-and, Andy, just coffee, Andy—cute, huh?
Mister, you don't know what it felt like,
Thinkin that was a nickel under my foot,
    She has been talking over music; now the tune
    carries her with it.
  Maybe you wonder what it is,
  Makes people good or bad;
  Why some guy, an ace without a doubt,

97

Turns out to be a bastard,
And the other way about.
I'll tell you what I feel:
It's just the nickel under the heel. . . .

Oh, you can live like Hearts-and-Flowers,
And every day is a wonderland tour.
Oh, you can dream and scheme
And happily put and take, take and put. . . .
But first be sure
The nickel's under your foot.

Go stand on someone's neck while you're takin;
Cut into somebody's throat as you put—
For every dream and scheme's
Depending on whether, all through the storm,
You've kept it warm. . . .
The nickel under your foot.

And if you're sweet, then you'll grow rotten;
Your pretty heart covered over with soot.
And if for once you're gay,
And devil-may-careless, and oh, so hot . . .
I know you've got
That nickel under your foot.
        The lights come up. The Cop *appears.*

Cop

Which of you guys wanted to see the man who made
    the speech?

NICKEL UNDER THE FOOT

Words and Music by Marc Blitzstein

Allegretto

MAY-BE YOU WON-DER WHAT IT IS MAKES PEOP-LE GOOD OR BAD; WHY SOME GUY, AN ACE WITH-OUT A DOUBT, TURNS OUT TO BE A BAST-ARD, AND THE OTH-ER WAY A - BOUT. I'LL TELL YOU WHAT I FEEL - IT'S JUST THE NICK-EL UN - DER THE HEEL_____ O YOU CAN

LIVE LIKE HEARTS AND FLOW-ERS_____ AND EVE-RY DAY IS A

WON-DER-LAND TOUR. O YOU CAN DREAM AND SCHEME AND

cresc.

HAP-PI-LY PUT AND TAKE, TAKE AND PUT_____ BUT FIRST BE

SURE_____ THE NICK-EL'S UN-DER YOUR FOOT._____

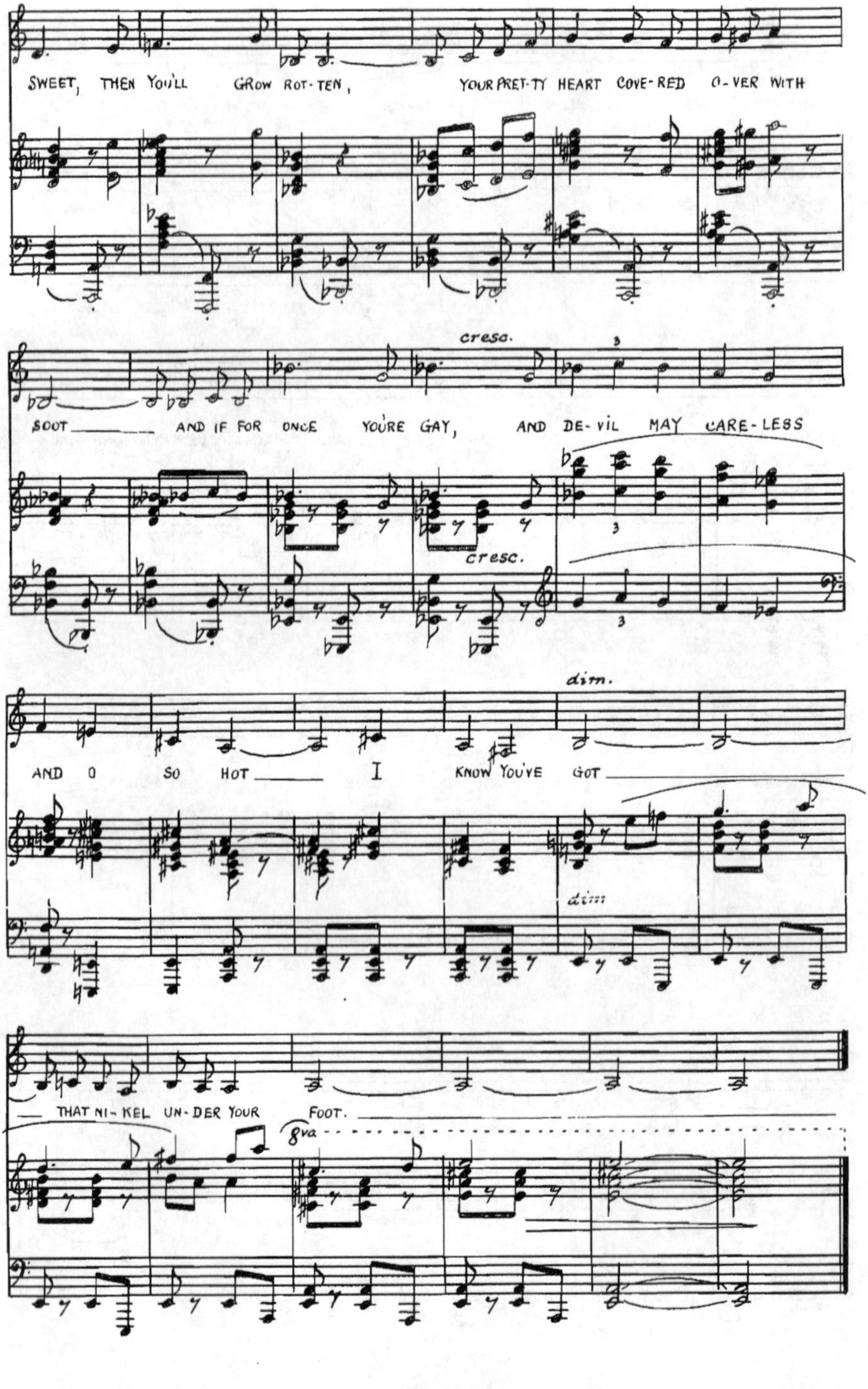
SWEET, THEN YOU'LL GROW ROT-TEN, YOUR PRET-TY HEART COVE-RED O-VER WITH
cresc.
SOOT AND IF FOR ONCE YOU'RE GAY, AND DE-VIL MAY CARE-LESS
cresc.
dim.
AND O SO HOT I KNOW YOU'VE GOT
dim
THAT NI-KEL UN-DER YOUR FOOT.
8va

Hey, Larry Foreman, now make a speech!
Instantly the LIBERTY COMMITTEE *is in a dither.*

REVEREND SALVATION

That's the man who made the speech!

REVEREND SALVATION AND DAUBER

He's the one who started this!

DR. SPECIALIST

Wait till Mr. Mister comes.

REVEREND SALVATION AND DAUBER

Did you phone to Mr. Mister?
What'd he say? What'd he say?

EDITOR DAILY

Mr. Mister's not at home.

YASHA, PREXY AND TRIXIE

Not at home?

EDITOR DAILY

At a meeting with the Board.

REVEREND SALVATION AND DAUBER

With the Board?

EDITOR DAILY

Says the Judge is with him, too.
He'll come over right away. . . .
Just as soon as they get through.

YASHA, PREXY AND TRIXIE

What'd he say? What'd he say?

REVEREND SALVATION AND DAUBER

He'll come over right away.
Enter LARRY FOREMAN.

DR. SPECIALIST

That's the man who made the speech!

REVEREND SALVATION AND DAUBER

He's the one who made the speech?

PREXY AND TRIXIE

He's the one who started this?

LARRY

*He has already started on a long note which
breaks.*
O-o-o-h, boy!
LARRY *is the hero of the piece. He's not
very good-looking—a humorous face, and an
engaging manner. Confidence is there, too; not*

104

*self-confidence; a kind of knowledge about the
way things probably have to work out. It gives
him a surprising modesty, and a young poise.*

I just been grilled. Say, who made up that word,
grilled? I also been barbecued, frizzled, and

Tries to sit.

pleated. Now I know what the dirty foreigners feel like.
I guess I am a foreigner at that. Our property's been in
the family for over sixty years. . . . But it's nine miles
outa town, so that makes me a foreigner. Not that it's
a good property. . . . If it was, we wouldn't have it no
sixty minutes. Ever hear of Mr. Mister? There's an
A-number-one homesnatcher; a lotta hard work and
perseverance went into that reputation. . . .

He turns, sees the LIBERTY COMMITTEE *all eyeing
him balefully.*

Saaay, what's the whole Liberty Committee doin in a
nightcourt? And on the wrong side of the bar? Wait
till I tell my Aunt Jessie . . . She's got a comeback for
everything. "Allus said they was the biggest cheats and
whores in town." Excuse the language, Miss,

To MOLL.

My Aunt Jessie gets all them big words outa the Bible.

Looks at her more closely.

You're new here. What's the matter, they catch you on
the streets, kid?

MOLL

Uh huh. Whatta they got you for?

LARRY

Who, me?
Makin a speech and passin out leaflets!
The fawmal chahge is Incitin to Riot—
Ain't you ever seen my act?
    He goes into it.
Well, I'm creepin along in the dark;
My eyes is crafty, my pockets is bulging!
I'm loaded, armed to the teeth—with leaflets.
And am I quick on the draw!
I come up to you . . . very slow . . . very snaky;
And with one fell gesture—
I tuck a leaflet in your hand.
And then, one, two, three—
There's a riot. You're the riot.
I incited you . . . I'm terrific, I am!

MOLL

That don't sound like nothin to get arrested for;
Besides, you don't seem very worried.

LARRY

Listen, girlie, you don't want to talk that way, that's
dangerous talk. First thing you know they'll have you
deported as well as fumigated. . . . But it's a good leaflet,
we printed it ourselves. We got a committee, too, farm-
ers and city people, doctors, lawyers, newspapermen, even
a couple of poets—and one preacher. We're middle class,

we all got property—we also got our eyes open. This
crowd here?
>*A chord.*

Hidin up there in the cradle of the Liberty Committee?
>*Another chord.*

Upon the topmost bough of yonder tree now,
Like bees in their hives,
The lords and their lackeys and wives—
A swingin "Rockabye Baby" in a nice big cradle.
Then they remark the air is chilly up there;
The sky beetle-browed; can that be a cloud over
there?
And then they put out their hands and feel stormy
weather!
A birdie ups and cries . . . "Boys, this looks bad;
You haven't used your eyes; you'll wish you had."

That's thunder, that's lightning,
And it's going to surround you!
No wonder those stormbirds
Seem to circle around you!
Well, you can't climb down, and you can't sit still;
That's a storm that's going to last until
The final wind blows . . . and when the wind
blows . . .
The cradle will rock!

That's thunder, that's lightning,
And it's going to surround you!

No wonder those stormbirds
Seem to circle around you!
Well, you can't climb down, and you can't say "No"!
You can't stop the weather, not with all your dough!
For when the wind blows . . . Oh, when the wind
blows . . .
The cradle will rock!

The cradle will rock! Do you think we don't know
what that fight tonight's about? Why Murphy from the
rolling mills and Brown from the roughers, and Young
from the boilermakers, is sittin together in Union Headquarters? Why more people than Steeltown ever saw
at one time are crowdin around in the square? Those
boys don't know it, but they're fightin our fight, too.
They're makin onions grow all over the land where
nothin but cactus grew before . . . and they'll have the
machinists and the blasters with 'em before the week is
out . . . try and stop 'em!

YASHA

Did he say onions?

DAUBER

Yes, but he means unions!

YASHA

O.

LARRY

Did you see the people . . . the tons of 'em? And the
order, the quiet? I lost my Aunt Jessie in a crowd of

THE CRADLE WILL ROCK

Words and Music by Marc Blitzstein

You hav-ent used your eyes, you'll wish you had._____ that's

thun - der, that's light - ning, and it's going to sur-round you!

No won - der those storm - birds seem to

circle a - round you!

I. Well you can't climb down and you
II. Well you can't climb down and you

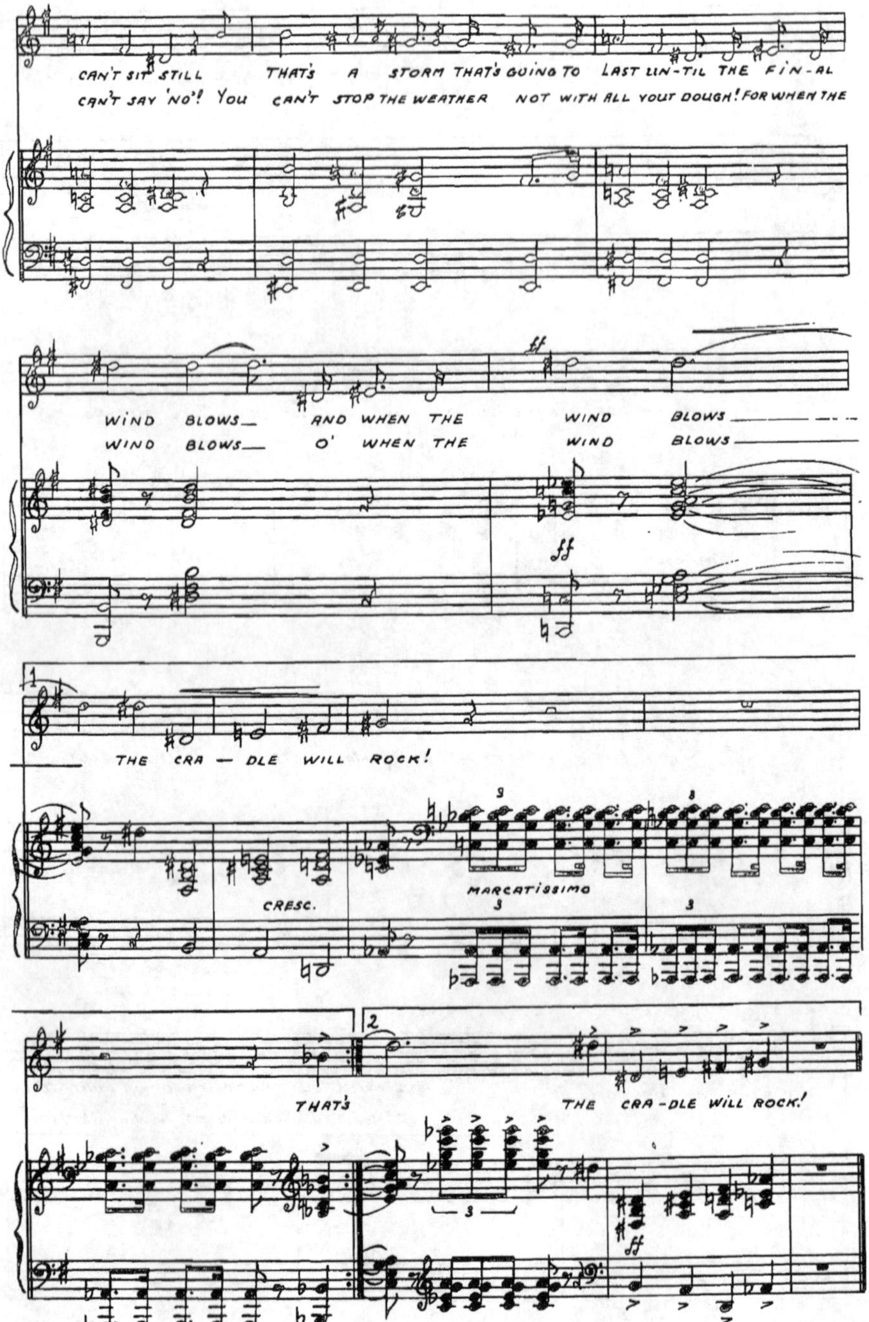
CAN'T SIT STILL THAT'S A STORM THAT'S GOING TO LAST UN-TIL THE FIN-AL
CAN'T SAY 'NO'! YOU CAN'T STOP THE WEATHER NOT WITH ALL YOUT DOUGH! FOR WHEN THE
WIND BLOWS— AND WHEN THE WIND BLOWS
WIND BLOWS— O' WHEN THE WIND BLOWS
ff
THE CRA — DLE WILL ROCK!
CRESC.
MARCATISSIMO
THAT'S THE CRA-DLE WILL ROCK!

boilermakers, bunched together with their wives and kids on one side of the square . . . the kids all had bugles! I'll find her blowin a bugle, I guess! Unless they pull her in for carryin concealed deadly leaflets—two-gun Jessie herself! Over on the other side of the square, the roughers with their kids . . . and their kids had drums.

DRUGGIST
I saw them. In the middle of the square were the rolling mill workers—their kids out in front too, with fifes.

LARRY
Do you know what it takes to keep a kid from blowin his bugle or bangin his drum? They're all there now, not makin a sound— Just waitin, waitin—ready to strike up the band as soon as they hear the good news.

DRUGGIST
I asked one little boy why he wasn't playin his fife— and he said to me, "Mister, that's discipline."

LARRY
Tonight's the night! O boy, if they get together! O boy, O boy, O boy! Good-bye, open shop in Steeltown! Hello, closed shop!

MOLL
Comes over and sits by him.
What's the difference?

LARRY

The difference? Open shop is when a boilermaker can be kicked around, demoted, fired, like that—he's all alone, he's free—free to be wiped out. Closed shop— he's got fifty thousand other boilermakers behind him, ready to back him up, every one of them, to the last lunch pail. The difference? It's like the five fingers on your hand.

That's

Tapping one finger.

the boilermakers—just one finger—but this—

Pointing to finger for each.

rollers, roughers, machinists, blasters, boilermakers— that's closed shop!

Makes a fist of it.

that's a union!

Thumbing nose with that hand.

O boy! O boy! O boy!

The LIBERTY COMMITTEE *seem curiously the target for the gesture.*

CLERK

Order in the courtroom!
Next case. Name?

PREXY

I am President Prexy of College University, and these are Professors Mamie and Trixie of the same institution.

CLERK

Charge?

LARRY

Imitating his Aunt Jessie.
Maintaining a disorderly house!

SCENE EIGHT

FACULTYROOM

PREXY *dozes at his desk. Telephone bell rings.*

PREXY

Yes? Mr. Mister? Well, good heavens, man, show
him in!

Enter MR. MISTER.

Mr. Mister!

MR. MISTER

President Prexy.

PREXY

Lovely morning!

MR. MISTER

It's raining.

PREXY

Oh, is it raining? I had no idea; well, of all things . . .

MR. MISTER

My wife's waiting for me. I'll come to the point at
    once. I need a speaker—one of your professors;
Someone who can put up a good front.

116

PREXY

We have lots of professors this year,
Who make lovely appearances. Just what kind of a
    man—?

MR. MISTER

Rally next Saturday night.
I'm extending your military tactics course.
Two years' compulsory training now.
Didn't they tell you?

PREXY

No, they didn't tell me. Heh, heh—heh—
    The last "heh" is rather sad.

MR. MISTER

Well, we're building up quite a nice little regiment.
You never know when you need 'em.
There was that Aliquippa strike in 1933.
The National Guard isn't any cheaper,
And I can handle college boys myself.

PREXY

Mmmmmm.

MR. MISTER

The country's going to the dogs,
What with the unions . . .

PREXY

Anxious to corroborate.
Mmmmmmmmmmm!

MR. MISTER

And sitdown strikes—
PREXY *"Ts-Ts-Ts"-es.*
Well, I want a professor from the University,
To come and talk to the students, stir 'em up—
Someone who can talk.

PREXY

Let me see, who would be the kind of man
Most suited to your purpose?
He thinks, then takes phone.
Send in Mamie, Scoot and Trixie.
Hangs up.
Mamie's a new one, just up from the Argentine;
He may be the very article!
MR. MISTER *grunts; takes out a newspaper.
Enter* MAMIE, SCOOT *and* TRIXIE. SCOOT, *whom
we haven't met yet, is the sort of eternally un-
washed bookworm who sits bespectacled in the
campus cafeteria utterly absorbed in his book,
probably Sanskrit.*

PREXY

Boys, this is Mr. Mister, our distinguished citizen—
and trustee. He—

Whispers.

Psssssst!

SCOOT, MAMIE AND TRIXIE

Psssst! Psssst! Psssst!

They go into a football huddle.

Ta dee, ta doo, ta da da da!

Ta dee, ta doo, ta da da da!

SCOOT

Trying to rise.

But, President Prexy, I feel—

PREXY

Pulls him down.

Not now, Scoot, you first, Mamie!

Police whistle.

MAMIE

Steps forward modestly.

Applied science, Laboratory 54.

Thinks hard.

Military training? Mmmmmmm.

Has an idea.

Young gentlemen of the University—

I give you—the Triple-Flank-Maneuver!

SCOOT

President Prexy, I still feel—

119

PREXY

Shhhhhh!

MAMIE

*He goes right on, hoping to heaven something
sensible will come out.*

That maneuver is a sort of symbol, a connection if you
will—

A connection so to speak with the times—

The times and the tides, the tides and the times as it
were!

Cloistered life—sanctum of learning—

Home of the Higher Good—Haven of the—uh—Humanities, the—

What shall I say?—The Humanities, in short!

Very brightly.

SCOOT

But—my dear sir!

PREXY

Scoot, your turn will come! Hush!

MAMIE

The University has a much broader *base* than many
people might give it credit for—having—a much—
broader—base.

Not so brightly, but still valiant.

May I, in conclusion, once again, as a sort of peroration,
without wishing to appear drastic, mind you, may I give

you, but also with no apologies, whatsoever, the Triple-
Flank-Maneuver?

MR. MISTER *shakes his head emphatically.*

PREXY
*Like the Madam whose first wench is discovered
to be bowlegged.*
Thank you, thank you, thank you, thank you. Wait.
We'll let you know.

MAMIE *to the side, huffily.*

MR. MISTER
Too many long words. What's he think college boys
are? They won't know he's talking about military training.

PREXY
Hopefully to Number Two.
Now, Professor Scoot!

SCOOT
Very stern; his chance has come!
Ethics 42, Esthetics 6, Logic 1.

PREXY
How do you feel about our course in military tactics?

SCOOT
A fateful pause.
Do I have to say?

PREXY

What now?
Why, yes.

SCOOT

Poisonously.
Then I don't like military training,
Military training of any kind!
I'm a Tolstoyan!

MR. MISTER, PREXY, MAMIE, TRIXIE
A *what?*

SCOOT
A Little Brother.

MR. MISTER

Bellowing.
Where were you during the war?

SCOOT
Henry Ford's Peace Ship.

MR. MISTER, PREXY, MAMIE, TRIXIE
A mixture of rage, amazement and despair.
O! O! O! O!

PREXY

O, I'm sorry!
How did he get on our payroll?
Believe me, he's off it now.
Why, Trixie!

122

TRIXIE

*Has been removing his turtle-neck sweater,
flings it on the floor, and stands in robust and
silly upper nakedness.*

Football Coach, also Elementary French . . .

He goes into his turn.

Listen, fellas!
Military course—two years?
Tree cheers! Listen, fellas!
Army training— Port in a storm!
There's nuttin like a uniform!
Soivice stripes—epaulettes—
Silver Shoit maybe—attababy!
Builds you up!—Alma Mater!
Sex Appeal!
Two years! Tree cheers!
Stick your chest out!
Be a man!

MR. MISTER

At last.

Wonderful! Wonderful!

PREXY

Beaming and helping TRIXIE *on with his sweater.*

Enchanting, enchanting, enchan*ting!*

MR. MISTER

You can both consider yourselves on my Liberty Committee.

123

MAMIE *peeks forward.*

I guess we can use Mamie too, those long words may come in handy there—but not that Peace Ship—!

SCOOT *snorts.*

Now you can tell the boys we're buying them the best military equipment—

The music gently goes lullaby.

Riot guns, tear gas, hand grenades, cartridges, everything —they're going to find that three or even four years of such training

Is not going to hurt—not going to hurt—

Not going to hurt—

SCENE NINE

DR. SPECIALIST'S OFFICE

MR. MISTER *being examined by* DR. SPECIALIST.

MR. MISTER
Not going to hurt, is it, Doctor?
It's not going to hurt?

DR. SPECIALIST
Now, don't be alarmed, old man,
A purely routine examination. . . .
Just breathe naturally.

MR. MISTER
It hurts sometimes when I breathe, Doc, you know.

DR. SPECIALIST
Where—here?
Tries various places.

MR. MISTER
No—not now, Doc. But it does hurt.

DR. SPECIALIST
Just breathe naturally.

125

MR. MISTER *breathes heavily, with fear.*
Mmmm. Mostly nerves. There are some new injections,
rather rare in this country. We'll start them tomorrow;
and remember—a long cure at Vichy this summer. I
think that's all.

MR. MISTER

All? You're certainly not forgetting to take my tem-
perature and pulse, Doctor?

DR. SPECIALIST

Suppressing a smile.
Fair enough.
Does so.
Incidentally, old man, I want to thank you for being
made chairman of the Liberty Committee. It means a
great deal to me, as you probably knew. Among other
things, I believe that's all I needed to get a research ap-
pointment I've been after for months.
Takes thermometer; looks at it.
Perfectly normal.

MR. MISTER

Really disappointed.
Normal?

DR. SPECIALIST

Completely. Pulse a bit jumpy. Just nerves, that's all.

ATTENDANT'S VOICE

Over desk-speaker.
Ella Hammer to see you, Doctor.

MR. MISTER

Ella Hammer?
That's the sister of the machinist who got hurt, isn't it?
What's she doing here?

DR. SPECIALIST

No idea. I treated him at the clinic.

MR. MISTER

He lights a cigar.
I think I know what she wants.
The man was drunk at the time, wasn't he?
Offers DR. SPECIALIST *a cigar.*

DR. SPECIALIST

Drunk? Why, no.
He also refuses the cigar.

MR. MISTER

On the alert, but revealing it.
No? That's very interesting. I was sure I heard he
    slipped
Because he had been drinking.

DR. SPECIALIST

Well . . . Is it causing you any trouble?

MR. MISTER

Easily.

Oh, in a sort of way. He's been trying to put over
This new union stuff on the employees. . . .
The kind that's never satisfied.
His sister's beefing all over the place
How he got pushed into that ladle. . . .

Rather humorously.

You know I had a hard time deciding whether a doctor
Was the right type to head a Liberty Committee; I
    decided—
Well, for a number of reasons. . . .
I assumed, naturally, after you examined him—
Didn't *you* say he was drunk?

DR. SPECIALIST

I . . . ?

MR. MISTER

A bit sharply.

Yes, you! As a matter of fact, I phoned the newspapers
only this morning to send someone over to get the story
from you. . . .

Humorous again.

I'm wondering how easily you could explain your sudden resignation as chairman of the Liberty Committee
to your extensive practice. . . . That is, if a change was
found advisable. . . .

*The cigar drops from his mouth; he is suddenly
a sort of maniac.*

128

Good God, I'm a sick man, Doctor! Doesn't anyone re-
alize how sick I am? I have nightmares, I'm in the middle of an earthquake! Call it nerves, call it what you
like! I don't understand the times . . . unions, unions . . .

He grinds the cigar under his heel.

We raised their wages, now they want a union! Things
are slipping from my grasp; what's it coming to? My
own doctor helps to make me sick!

He calms down.

There, you see.

Brokenly, and with great charm.

I guess you can handle her, eh?

There is a long pause. MR. MISTER, *completely
recovered, leaves. On the way he meets* ELLA
HAMMER *coming in. They stare at each other,
then* MR. MISTER *looks once again at* DR. SPE-
CIALIST, *and departs.*

ELLA

*She wears a tam and windbreaker. She is no
longer young; right now she is in dead earnest.*

Hello, Doctor.

Doctor, you examined Joe—

Doctor, you're the one to know;

If he ever touched a drop of liquor,

He couldn't hold it. You know his stomach.

They take enough out of his paycheck

For you to know his stomach by now!

DR. SPECIALIST
He taps twice with his pencil.
Yes.

ELLA
Is the rumor true that they
Mean to say that he was drunk?

DR. SPECIALIST
The pencil taps.
Yes.

ELLA
But, Doctor, you know those hoodlums framed him!
Pushed him into that ladle
Because he wasn't afraid to talk!
He's been expecting this for weeks!
He even told *you* that!

DR. SPECIALIST
The pencil taps.
Yes.

ELLA
Workers who have been cheated and lied to and sold
    out—
They daren't trust anybody no more!
They mustn't lose their faith in Joe, now—
You see that, don't you?
Her voice rises. No tears, only fury.

130

Dr. Specialist
The pencil taps.
Yes.

Ella
His last "yes" disarms her. Somewhat more quietly.
So—you will tell the workers it was all a frameup . . .
You'll say their confidence in him was not unfounded?
I hoped you would.

Attendant's Voice
Reporters from the newspapers, sir.

Dr. Specialist
The pencil taps.
Yes.
Enter two Reporters.

Reporter One
Good morning, Doctor.

Reporter Two
Mr. Mister phoned us to come here; we aren't quite
sure what for.
A pause.

Dr. Specialist
*Finally he speaks. He looks steadily down at
something on his desk.*

131

Gentlemen, I'll be brief. My statement is this: I examined the man Hammer shortly after his injury at the Steeltown mills last Thursday. He was obviously intoxicated.

> ELLA *shoots a swift glance at him.*

That is all.

REPORTER ONE

But, Doctor, isn't there any more?

REPORTER TWO

That hardly makes a complete story.

ELLA

> *Steps forward; so quietly you have to strain to hear her.*

A story? Is that what your papers want, a story?

Listen, here's a story.
Not much fun, and not much glory;
Lowclass . . . lowdown. . . .
The thing you never care to see,
Until there is a showdown.
Here it is—I'll make it snappy:
Are you ready? Everybody happy?

Joe Worker gets gypped;
For no good reason, just gypped,
From the start until the finish comes . . .
They feed him out of garbage cans,

JOE WORKER

Words and Music by Marc Blitzstein

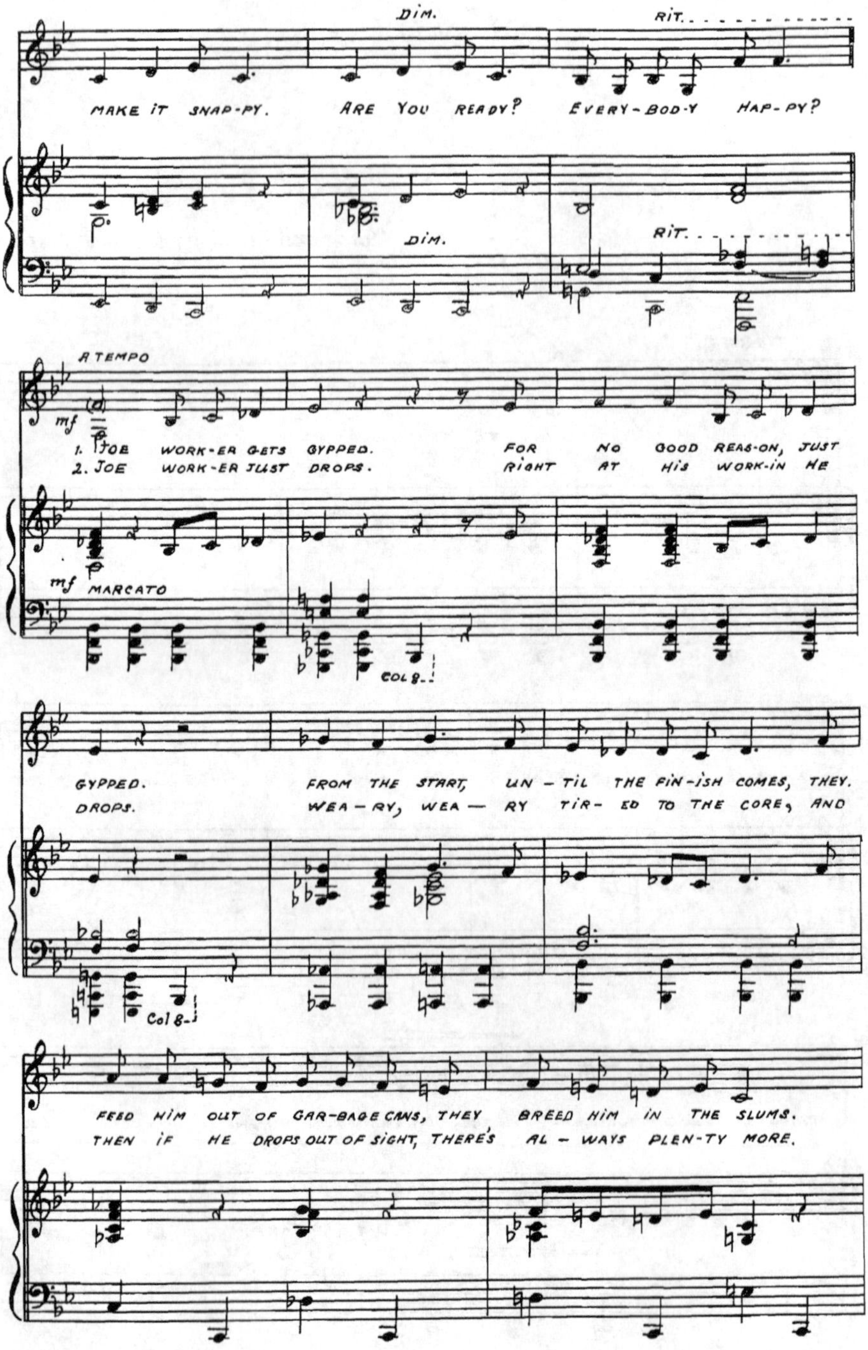
DIM.
RIT.
MAKE IT SNAP-PY. ARE YOU READY? EVERY-BOD-Y HAP-PY?
DIM.
RIT.
A TEMPO
mf
1. JOE WORK-ER GETS GYPPED. FOR NO GOOD REAS-ON, JUST
2. JOE WORK-ER JUST DROPS. RIGHT AT HIS WORK-IN HE
mf MARCATO
Col 8
GYPPED. FROM THE START, UN-TIL THE FIN-ISH COMES, THEY
DROPS. WEA-RY, WEA-RY TIR-ED TO THE CORE, AND
Col 8
FEED HIM OUT OF GAR-BAGE CANS, THEY BREED HIM IN THE SLUMS.
THEN IF HE DROPS OUT OF SIGHT, THERE'S AL-WAYS PLEN-TY MORE.

JOE WORK-ER WILL GO TO SHOPS WHERE STUFF IS ON
JOE WORK-ER MUST KNOW THAT SOME-BOD-YS GOT HIM IN

SHOW, HE'LL LOOK AT THE MEAT, HE'LL LOOK AT THE BREAD AND TOO
TOW. BUT WHAT IS THE GOOD FOR ONE TO BE CLEAR? O, IT

LIT-TLE TO EAT SORT OF GOES TO THE HEAD
TAKES A LOT OF JOES TO MAKE A SOUND YOU CAN HEAR!

CRESC. RIT.
ONE BIG QUES-TION IN — SIDE ME CRIES:
ONE BIG QUES-TION IN — SIDE ME CRIES:
CRESC. RIT

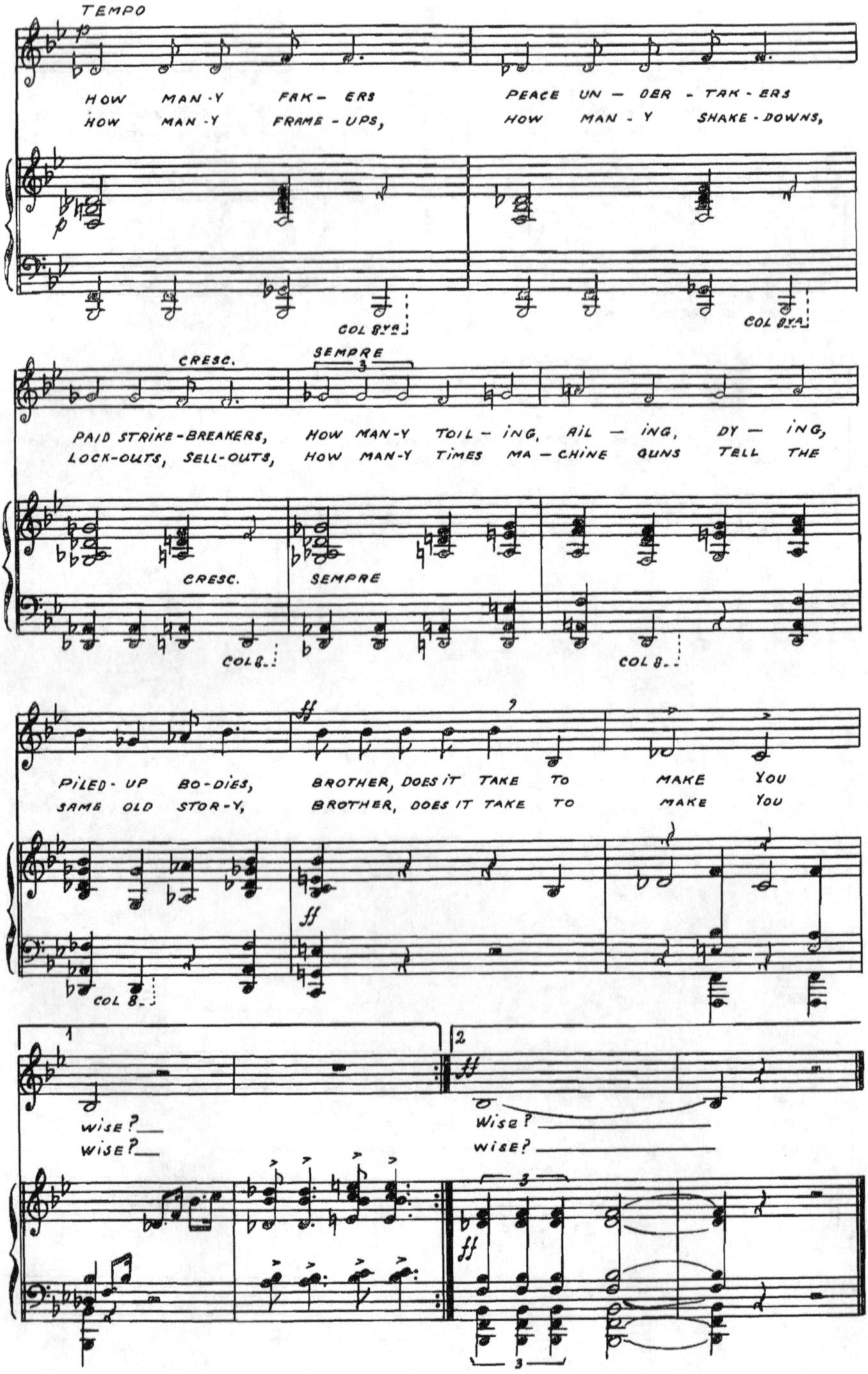
TEMPO
HOW MAN-Y FAK-ERS PEACE UN-DER-TAK-ERS
HOW MAN-Y FRAME-UPS, HOW MAN-Y SHAKE-DOWNS,
COL 8VA
COL 8VA
CRESC.
SEMPRE
PAID STRIKE-BREAKERS, HOW MAN-Y TOIL-ING, AIL-ING, DY-ING,
LOCK-OUTS, SELL-OUTS, HOW MAN-Y TIMES MA-CHINE GUNS TELL THE
CRESC.
SEMPRE
COL 8
COL 8
PILED-UP BO-DIES, BROTHER, DOES IT TAKE TO MAKE YOU
SAME OLD STOR-Y, BROTHER, DOES IT TAKE TO MAKE YOU
COL 8
WISE?
WISE?
WISE?
WISE?

THE CRADLE WILL ROCK

They breed him in the slums!
Joe Worker will go,
To shops where stuff is on show;
He'll look at the meat,
He'll look at the bread,
And too little to eat sort of goes to the head.
One big question inside me cries:
How many fakers, peace undertakers,
Paid strikebreakers,
How many toiling, ailing, dying, piledup bodies,
Brother, does it take to make you wise?

Joe Worker just drops,
Right at his workin he drops,
Weary, weary, tired to the core;
And then if he drops out of sight there's always plenty
      more!
Joe Worker must know
That somebody's got him in tow. . . .
Yet what is the good
For just one to be clear?
Oh, it takes a lot of Joes
To make a sound you can hear!
One big question inside me cries:
How many frameups, how many shakedowns,
Lockouts, sellouts,
How many times machine guns tell the same old story,
Brother, does it take to make you wise?

SCENE TEN

NIGHTCOURT

LARRY
And so the great Dr. Specialist drew a research appointment, and kept his job on the Liberty Committee.

MOLL
Gee, and I thought they were all so high class!

LARRY
Sister, you should be ashamed—an amateur like you in the company of all these professionals? They could teach you something. For instance, you'll probably go to jail. . . . But do you think they will?
Not on your committee button, they won't!

PREXY
Will Mr. Mister never get here?

YASHA
It seems we've been here *hours!*

REVEREND SALVATION
I insist that man be stopped. He's already caused enough trouble. What is this, Russia? We don't have to listen to talk like that!

THE CRADLE WILL ROCK

LARRY

No, you don't have to listen.
You're all independent, you are;
There ain't no Mr. Mister, there's just the bogey man.
You preach what he tells you to preach. . . .
You print what he tells you to print . . . or else!
You sell out everything you got . . .
Your store, your son, yourself.

DRUGGIST

Stevie!

LARRY

Mr. Mister comes around, and you . . .
Kiss the ground where he walks.
Mrs. Mister lifts a finger, and you . . .
Lift your little behind to be smacked!
This ain't Russia, no . . . it's Steeltown, U. S. A.!

DAUBER

What do you want us to do, join unions?

PREXY

A University President's Union!

YASHA

A Concert Artists' Union!

LIBERTY COMMITTEE

Don't make us laugh!

139

DRUGGIST

I got some sort of invitation to join a pharmacists' union—I wonder if they know there's a poolroom now where my drugstore was.

LARRY

Didn't anyone ever tell you boys you belong to a union already?

Derision from the LIBERTY COMMITTEE.

It's the closedest shop ever heard of—and it's been runnin things for quite a while. Only you're bein rooked; You're in one of them racketeer unions, where you run all the errands and get maybe a dollar cigar for Christmas. You ain't made one real demand yet, you've only said, "Yes, Mr. Mister," up to now. You're caught there, boys; you're stuck like a sandwich between the top crowd pressin down and the bottom crowd comin up! What do you wanna be, hamburgers? I ask you!

He makes a gesture to the LIBERTY COMMITTEE.
Enter MR. MISTER, *haggard, pale.*

LIBERTY COMMITTEE

Mr. Mister!

Rushes to him.

You got here at last!

Oh, you don't know what we've been through!

These idiots don't know us!

Hurry! Get us out! Now that you've come . . . etc., etc.

MR. MISTER *passes through them, goes straight to* LARRY.

140

MR. MISTER

You're Larry Foreman?

LARRY

Ex-foreman.

MR. MISTER

I've been looking all over town for you.

LARRY

Well, how's the union returns?

MR. MISTER

They haven't come to a decision yet. Mr. Foreman, I know a lot about you, you were once in my employ. Look here . . . We're both for the same thing, a fair and square deal for everybody. Why don't you persuade your group to join with the Liberty Committee into one big united organization?

LARRY

On guard, non-committal.
You mean with these people here?

MR. MISTER

Yes, a bad mistake, their being here.
To CLERK.
Release them at once. I told the Judge to go on home, I have his authority. That includes you, too, Mr. Foreman, of course.

141

LARRY

You got his authority, eh?

MR. MISTER

Yes, my brother-in-law, you know.

LARRY

Oh, the Judge is your brother-in-law. He's part of the Liberty Committee, too?

MR. MISTER

And some of the best people in town. Dr. Specialist over there . . . Editor Daily, you know him . . . and they're all very democratic. Come now, what do you say?

LARRY

Let me understand you. . . . You'd like my services in swinging your way all the people I've signed up— All the people who agree with union. You want me to change their mind, is that it?

MR. MISTER

Well, that's a little strongly put.

LARRY

Oh, Mr. Mister, you can be perfectly frank with me.

LIBERTY COMMITTEE

That's it! That's it! Now do it!

DRUGGIST

No, don't!

LIBERTY COMMITTEE

Go ahead!
Go ahead!

MOLL

Starts humming verse of "Nickel Under the Foot."

Oh, you can live like hearts and flowers,

MR. MISTER

When all this trouble's over, I'll see to it personally that there's a wave of increased production, improved methods, closer competition than the country's ever seen. Do they know I'm building them a swimming pool? A library? A private park for their children?

LARRY

From where I sit it looks like they only want a union.

MR. MISTER

I don't want to talk about your own future. There's nothing you

And every day is a
wonderland tour,
Oh, you can dream
and scheme, and
happily put and
take, take and put
But first be . . .

DRUGGIST

No, don't do it!

sure
The nickel's under
your
foot.
Go stand on some-
one's neck while
you're takin,

LIBERTY COMMITTEE

Listen, you!

couldn't be. I haven't time to argue. Well?

LARRY
I might, but it's a tall order you know.

MR. MISTER
Well, of course, I don't expect you to do it just like that.

LARRY
Ought to be worth quite a sum to you, eh?

MR. MISTER
I thought so. You needn't worry about that part. I'll see you get what it's worth. Let's talk it over outside.

That's Mr. Mister . . .

Mr. Mister!
And that's an offer he's making you!

Take it!
Like it!

He's making you an offer, making you an offer! Do you understand?

DRUGGIST
Don't do it!

Remember,

A murderer!
Like me—
Watch your step, boy!

Cut into somebody's throat as you
Put

For every dream and

Scheme's depending on whether all through the storm, You've kept it warm—

the nickel under your foot.

145

LARRY
Wait! I'm kinda funny that way. I'd like to know now about how much it might be worth?

MR. MISTER *writes a figure on a slip of paper and hands it to* LARRY

Go on, go on, you son-of-a-bitch, you lousy foreman, who do you think you are? Go on, go on! that's Mr. Mister! Making you an offer! Take it! Take it! Making you an offer! Mr. Mister!

No!

Stop him!
I know! I care!
Wait! Wait!
I can't stand it!

And if you're sweet, then
You'll grow rotten;
Your pretty heart covered over with soot
—And if for once you're gay and devil-may-careless and
O, so hot,—I know you've got—

THE CRADLE WILL ROCK

LARRY

Through the silence which follows the last words.

You don't say. Worth that much to you, hm?
Well, you take all that money and go buy yourself
A big piece of toast.
You wanna relax—and to me and my Aunt Jessie,
You're a poached egg.

MR. MISTER

What?

LIBERTY COMMITTEE

Fool! Fool!

DRUGGIST

Stevie!

LARRY

Now, then, get outa here;
And take this little girl with you!
Out there she doesn't cost you nothin—
In jail you're liable to have to feed her!

MR. MISTER

Why, you Goddamned skunk!
I'll break you . . . I'll run you out of town. . . .

LARRY

And give us front page publicity? Would you? Please?

LIBERTY COMMITTEE

Kill him! Lynch him!

147

LARRY

Yeh, lynch, kill!
Listen once for all, you scared bunch of ninnies!
Outside in the square they're startin somethin
That's gonna tear the catgut outa your stinkin rackets!
That's *Steel* marchin out in front! but one day there's
    gonna be
    Wheat . . . and sidewalks . . .
    Cows . . . and music . . . .
    Shops . . . houses . . .
    Poems . . . bridges . . . drugstores . . .
The people of this town are findin out what it's all
    about . . .
They're growin up!
And when everybody gets together
Like Steel's gettin together tonight,
Where are you then?
Listen, you Black Legions, you Ku Kluxers,
You Vigil-Aunties hidin up there
In the Cradle of the Liberty Committee. . . .
When the storm breaks. . . .
    Quietly.
The cradle will fall!
    They watch his pointing hand descend slowly.
    Blare of bugles outside, left.
Listen! The boilermakers are with us! That's the boiler-
    makers' kids!
    Beat of drums, and the sound of voices singing
    "Upon the topmost bough."*

LARRY

The roughers!
Sound of fifes and more voices.

LARRY

The rollers! Steel! Your steel! They done it!
All the music and voices come nearer, back-stage and in the theatre too, converging upon the aisles. The LIBERTY COMMITTEE *are frozen where they stand.*

COP

They're marchin down here! They got no permit to march!

CLERK

Arrest them!

COP

Arrest them? There's thousands of 'em! They're standin in front of the courthouse, right here!

MR. MISTER

The surrender to fear.
My God! What do they want with me?

LARRY

Almost sheepishly.
Don't worry, that's not for you. That's just my Aunt Jessie and her committee.
Joins in with the song and music.

149

THE CRADLE WILL ROCK

That's thunder, that's lightning,
And it's going to surround you!
No wonder those stormbirds
Seem to circle around you. . . .
Well, you can't climb down, and you can't sit still;
That's a storm that's going to last until
The final wind blows . . . and when the wind blows . . .
The cradle will rock!
  Music, bugles, drums and fifes.

  Curtain

CPSIA information can be obtained
at www.ICGtesting.com
Printed in the USA
BVHW061937170419
545817BV00009B/289/P